ENGLISH DRAWINGS

AND WATERCOLORS 1550–1850

ENGLISH
DRAWINGS AND
WATERCOLORS
1550-1850

IN THE COLLECTION OF

MR. AND MRS. PAUL MELLON

THE PIERPONT MORGAN LIBRARY

HARPER & ROW · PUBLISHERS

TABLE OF CONTENTS

ALPHABETICAL LIST OF THE ARTISTS

FOREWORD

THESE 150 drawings and watercolors have been chosen to illustrate the achievement in English draughtsmanship over three hundred years, from the middle of the sixteenth century to the beginning of Victorian and Pre-Raphaelite art. They range from the work of artists such as Le Moyne, Wyck, and Hollar (who came to England from France or Holland or Bohemia, and brought with them a strong sense of European drawing and coloring) to Lear, Lewis, Ruskin, and their contemporaries, who spent many of their years abroad, recording the landscapes not only of France and Italy but also of Egypt, the Holy Land, India, and Ceylon. To make plain the development of eighteenth-century topographical drawing we have included Canaletto, who spent eight or nine years in England and helped to establish an English school of landscape art. After 1750 one can see decidedly English characteristics in every kind of drawing and watercolor, and the English school comes into its own and even begins to influence watercolor painting in France. Though a long sweep of the historical development of English art is shown here, four fifths of the drawings come from the years between 1750 and 1850, when the English genius in drawing and painting flowered.

The greatest masters are strongly represented, and the variety of their work and the course of their careers can be traced in the works which we have chosen. There are twelve drawings and watercolors by Turner, seven by Constable, six each by Blake and Palmer, and groups by Rowlandson, Gainsborough, Girtin, J. R. Cozens, and Paul Sandby. The works, however, have not been presented primarily to explain the changes in the evolution of draughtsmanship over three centuries of English art, or in the lives of the most brilliant and original artists, but because of their outstanding quality.

Mr. and Mrs. Mellon's collection of British art will be established at Yale University as part of a center for British art and British studies. Hitherto, the collection has been known chiefly through its paintings, although drawings were included in exhibitions in Washington, D.C., Richmond (Virginia), in London, and at Yale. In the last decade the collection has grown above all in size and distinction in drawings and watercolors of the period of this book. There are now more than three thousand, many of which are as yet unknown or very little known to the public. Less than a third of the works illustrated here has been previously reproduced; about two thirds of the drawings in this book have never been seen in the United States.

In this publication we have tried to present something of the history of English drawing and watercolor painting. Brief lives of the artists attempt to point out their individual characteristics; the illustrations are of such quality that the various techniques of the artists should be immediately clear.

The selection of works was made by Mr. John Baskett and Mr. Dudley Snelgrove, with

ix

me, and was approved by Mr. Mellon. Mr. Mellon has shown great interest in every aspect of this publication and in the exhibition of these drawings at The Pierpont Morgan Library, The Royal Academy, and at Yale. Most of the book was written by Mr. Baskett and Mr. Snelgrove. Their chief aide—one should say more fairly, their co-worker—has been Mrs. Judy Egerton, who has written part of the catalogue, checked hundreds of facts, and graciously assisted us in every way. We are indebted to Mr. Graham Reynolds, Keeper of the Department of Prints and Drawings and Paintings, Victoria and Albert Museum, for writing the introduction which surveys these three hundred years of English art. We are grateful to Mr. Evelyn Joll for writing the biography and notes for J. M. W. Turner, to Mr. John Harris for writing the biography and note for Sir James Thornhill, to Dr. Martin Butlin for writing the biography for William Blake. The notes for Blake's watercolors and drawings were my responsibility. Mrs. Patricia Jaffé provided information concerning George Romney and wrote the note about his drawing. Special information was given by Dr. John Hayes, Mr. Paul Hulton, Mr. David Greysmith, Mr. Oliver Millar, Mr. Anthony Reed, and Dr. Robert R. Wark. The expert work necessary in preparing the drawings for mounting was carried out by Brigadier David Tighe-Wood. Miss Margot Holloway gave valuable help in reading the proofs. Mr. Joseph Blumenthal, Mr. Joseph M. Bernstein, and Mr. John F. Peckham have assisted us extraordinarily in the design and printing of this book. Miss Beverly Carter has been invaluable in co-ordinating the shipment of the art between countries and for photographic reproductions. She has been assisted by Miss Michelle Charbonnet and Mr. Michael Markham. Professor Jules Prown and Mr. Kenneth Nesheim of Yale University, Mr. Peter Davidock of the National Gallery of Art, Washington, and Mrs. Patricia Reyes, Miss Nancy Russ, Miss Denise Whitney, and Mr. Alexander Jensen Yow of The Pierpont Morgan Library have provided special assistance.

All of these have made possible an international exhibition and publication which demonstrate the remarkable accomplishment within one school of art. We trust that English drawings and watercolors will be better known and more deeply appreciated because of this presentation of Mr. and Mrs. Mellon's collection.

CHARLES RYSKAMP
Director, The Pierpont Morgan Library

INTRODUCTION

WRITING IN 1762, Horace Walpole observed that England had rarely given birth to a genius in the pictorial arts: "Flanders and Holland have sent us the greatest men that we can boast." In the age of Hogarth he was, however, optimistic about the future of the national school, and the subsequent eruption of the most brilliant period in British painting justified his confidence. This sequence of events has suggested to many people that British art offers little of interest before the mid-eighteenth century. It is one of the merits of this wide-ranging and well-balanced selection of drawings and watercolors from the collection of Mr. and Mrs. Paul Mellon that it places the later and admittedly more original works in the context of their past, and enables us to trace the continuity and the national flavor of post-Renaissance art in England back to its origins in the sixteenth and seventeenth centuries.

Its dependence at that time on European models, and often on European masters, is neatly illustrated by the earliest work here, *A Young Daughter of the Picts* by Jacques Le Moyne de Morgues. This is the work of a French émigré artist who had been employed in America, and was engraved for a German publisher in order to show "that the Inhabitants of the great Bretannie have been in times past as savage as those of Virginia." The flowers which adorn the girl's body, apparently to show her unmarried status, echo the love of natural history seen in Elizabethan embroidery and countless drawings of garden flowers. The technique of minute stippling closely parallels the miniature painting which was flourishing at the time in the hands of Nicholas Hilliard and Isaac Oliver. Oliver himself repeats this cosmopolitan approach. Though born in France, his early artistic training as a portrait miniaturist seems to have been acquired in England; his style then matured through visits to the Netherlands and, even more significantly, to Venice. The particular formality of his *Leda and the Swan*, echoing an established pattern of mythological illustration, is not one which recurs frequently in English drawing over the next hundred years, though we find it again in Thornhill's allegory-laden Baroque.

The patrons of art always had a preference for contemporary fact, and this is reflected in the greater proportion of portraiture and landscape which has come down from the seventeenth century. The dominance of foreign-born artists is still marked. Wenceslaus Hollar was born in Bohemia and made his career in England in the wake of Lord Arundel's patronage, working "with a pretty spiritt." Both he and the Dutchman Thomas Wyck are seen in this collection recording significant areas of the metropolis of London. New buildings and the development of urban growth long remained subjects of pictorial interest, a later example here being Thomas Malton's study of the construction of the Adelphi.

As the natural tastes of the country developed and as they came more and more to be interpreted by native-born artists, certain predilections came to be emphasized. These included the love of open-air life and its accompaniments, the love of sport and the love of animals, and the observation of living people engaged in the normal activities of everyday life. The relative facility of drawing as opposed to oil painting enabled a group of draughtsmen to depict scenes of this nature which they might see around them with that air of informality which was then one of the most winning and unusual characteristics of their art. This engaging quality is anticipated here in Francis Barlow's lively seventeenth-century hare hunt, and can be savored in such diverse works as Lens's figures stiffly posed against the Long Water at Hampton Court, and Marcellus Laroon's scene of gallantry. The same quality inheres in Hogarth's moralities loaded with anecdote, and Hayman's game of shuttlecock in a grand interior. The fact that this kind of narrative painting flourished at the time when Richardson and Fielding were founding the English novel was recognized at the outset, and both the literary and the pictorial breakthrough correspond to a strong desire in the British to overcome the restrictions of academic custom.

The main stream of British watercolor painting began to flow at about the same time. Hitherto watercolor, or its opaque version, body color, had only been used sporadically as an adjunct to drawing in the more general sense. From the middle of the eighteenth century, with all the force of a great movement, fully pigmented watercolors were produced by a large number of artists, some of whom did not even work in oils. Many of these watercolor painters turned their eyes primarily on the scenery of the British Isles with the enthusiasm expressed by Walpole in his essay "On Modern Gardening": "If wood, water, groves, valleys, glades, can inspire poet or painter, this is the country, or this is the age to produce them." But in doing so they did not forget that it was inhabited by real people, and they preferred to show the inhabitants of their own day rather than mythological beings from Greece or Rome. In Rooker's watercolor the haymakers are seen drinking their small beer in the shadow of the Greyfriars chapel; in Dayes's drawing workpeople and beggars go about their business in the presence of the elegant inhabitants of Queen Square. Paul Sandby's *Rosslyn Castle* is typical of this current of British taste. The fashionable lady is making her drawing in a picturesque valley, dominated by the great bulk of the ancient castle. Painting watercolors was a craze with amateurs in the late eighteenth century, and their enthusiasm, sharpened by their experience of the difficulties of the process, encouraged them to patronize the professionals represented in this exhibition.

The mood of such stay-at-home works is serene, and combines matter-of-fact appreciation of the domestic realities of modern life with love of the English countryside and a gentle nostalgia for the past. But in the age in which Romanticism was born other artists felt and expressed stronger emotions towards landscape. Many of these artists found the subject matter which was most sympathetic to them by traveling through Switzerland to Italy. In this way they encountered mountain scenery of a grandeur unknown in the British Isles; they were thrilled by the monuments of antiquity and they met in Rome a cosmopolitan group who were interested in the same themes. This was the experience of Richard Wilson, Alexander Cozens, William Pars, and John "Warwick" Smith. This contrasted aspect of late eighteenth-century drawing reaches its climax in the sensational linear distortions of Francis Towne and the highly charged melancholy of John Robert Cozens. Other topographical draughtsmen sought or were sent to find exotic scenes in the most distant parts of the known world—Webber in the South Seas and Alaska, William Alexander in China, Chinnery in India and Macao, Samuel Daniell in Africa.

Not all late eighteenth-century draughtsmen were committed to landscape. Illustration and subject pictures abounded. The upsurge in the national school had encouraged an ambition towards the Grand Manner, large figurative compositions painted in imitation of the Old Masters. This effort was another characteristic of the Romantic Movement, which directed the artists' search for subjects towards those in which violent emotion and extravagant gesture might be appropriate. It was reflected in drawing as much as in the more ambitious media. Even a group of students studying a map in John Brown's *Geographers* is full of a sense of menace, and this histrionic approach is intensified in Romney's swirling wash drawing of a woman escaping from a city on fire and, to a still wilder pitch, in Fuseli's *Ariadne Watching the Struggle of Theseus with the Minotaur.*

Though he remains outside this world with his own symbolism and mode of expression, William Blake reflects the same body of literary ideas. In his entirely personal style he illustrates biblical themes, medieval history, and contemporary pastoral with a repertory of forms derived as much from Michelangelo as from the Gothic. But variety in approach and style is one of the chief attractions of British art in the late eighteenth century, and Rowlandson is at a diametrically opposed pole from his contemporary Blake, giving a good-humored and basically convincing picture of town and country life in his tinted outline drawings which verge on caricature. Thomas Girtin, whose almost abstract sense of structure in landscape is so strongly represented in this selection, stands at the culmination of yet another strand in British drawing, which had its roots in Flemish antecedents and grew through the influence of Canaletto and J. R. Cozens.

The increasing differentiation of watercolor painting as a department of British art in its own right in the nineteenth century, and the growing specialization of its practitioners, was formally marked by the establishment of the "Old" Watercolour Society in 1804. The watercolors selected for exhibition at this period would look strange to our eyes, crammed together as they were in heavy gilt frames and emulating oils in their size and range of color. Even so the exhibitors had found that they were competing against heavy disadvantages when they sent their work to the leading mixed exhibition at the Royal Academy, and that they had much to gain by segregating their wares; hence their secession to a Society of their own. It was speedily apparent that there was a distinct public interested in seeing and buying watercolors when shown in this way; and this fact was recognized by the formation of a second "New Society of Painters in Miniature and Watercolours" three years later. The volume of watercolors produced in England throughout the nineteenth century was greatly increased by these associations and their efforts on behalf of the medium. To them specialists such as John Varley, David Cox, and Peter De Wint owed their livelihood, and large collections, forerunners of the existing ones, began to come into existence.

Turner, who dominated watercolor painting as thoroughly as he dominated oil painting in the first half of the nineteenth century, stood aloof from these developments. He had made his reputation through the drawings he had exhibited at the Royal Academy from the age of fifteen. He continued to exhibit watercolors there long after he had transferred his main ambition to oil painting, and showed large groups in his own gallery and in some dealers' shops. In them he expressed his sense of the titanic forces of nature, and also the inexhaustible variety of scenery, color, and light with which he had become acquainted. With consummate skill he exploited every device possible to the medium and made use of every accidental effect. He found watercolor ideal for the exploration of a private world in which he could work out his ideas on color abstracted in large measure from the forms of the visible world.

In finding watercolor appropriate to these private meditations, Turner was continuing a well-founded tradition. Gainsborough, arranging coals, sand, and pieces of broccoli on an oak table, was a forerunner in drawing landscapes of the mind. And the strain continues throughout the nineteenth century. The work of Samuel Palmer's which appeals most strongly to us now was kept by him in *The Curiosity Portfolio*, shown only to a few of his most intimate friends. This ductility of watercolor enabled Richard Dadd to employ his artistic talent with imaginative effect after he had withdrawn into the even more constricted world of madness.

But the main outlets for British watercolor paintings in the nineteenth century came through their public appeal. It was Cotman's misfortune that, although uniquely gifted with a touch for the precise control of watercolor washes and significant edges, allied to an instinct for harmonious, transparent color, he never enjoyed popular support for his most individual productions. Other happier artists throve under brisk patronage. Some became for a time an influence on the Continent, instead of being recipients of influence. Bonington, working in Paris with what was regarded as a purely English medium, induced Delacroix, who greatly admired his lightness and fluency, to take up watercolor. And since the English were traveling in ever increasing numbers, there was a great demand for views of the most popular scenic attractions within their range. Wales remained a perennially popular subject throughout the nineteenth century, but the middle classes were beginning to travel outside their own islands. The drawings of picturesque places — a turreted window at Coblenz, the square at Innsbruck — or prints from them, were the equivalent of the modern travel agents' brochures. For instance, John Ruskin records how his father brought home Prout's *Sketches in Flanders and Germany*, "and as my mother watched my father's pleasure in looking at the wonderful places, she said why should we not go and see some of them in reality? My father hesitated a little, then with glittering eyes said — why not?" And so Ruskin himself was taken on the tour of Europe, and repaid his debt to the artists he admired by his own admirably spontaneous sketches of Swiss Alpine and Italian scenes.

Provided that they are selected with a sufficiently catholic taste, as they are here, it will be found that English watercolor painting exhibits as much variety and liveliness in the middle of the nineteenth century as it had done fifty years before. Its scope extended beyond the production of formal landscapes representing places at home and abroad, diversified by some more intimate productions of the secluded imagination. There were still many artists such as James Ward and J. F. Lewis making informal sketches in natural history. And there were many travelers to exotic scenes beyond the ordinary tourist's reach — Roberts to Egypt, Lear to the Balkans and further afield.

In fact, the movement which had been growing in scope and public acceptance over the last hundred years had reached its climax by 1850. Shortly afterwards its course was altered when the Pre-Raphaelites began to use watercolor as though it were interchangeable with oil, or used both methods in the same drawing. The successors to the grand epoch illustrated here are to be found as much in a cosmopolitan setting — Boudin, Whistler, Harpignies, Winslow Homer — as in the later history of the purely national school.

GRAHAM REYNOLDS

Keeper of the Department of Prints and Drawings and Paintings, Victoria and Albert Museum

BIBLIOGRAPHY

Frederick Antal. *Fuseli Studies*, 1956.

———. *Hogarth and his place in European Art*, 1962.

Sir Walter Armstrong. *Turner*, 1902.

John Baskett. *Constable Oil Sketches*, 1966.

R. B. Beckett, edited by. *John Constable's Correspondence*, 7 vols., Suffolk Records Society, 1962–70.

C. F. Bell and T. Girtin. *The Drawings and Sketches of John Robert Cozens*, Walpole Society, vol. XXIII, 1935.

G. E. Bentley, Jr. *Blake Records*, 1969.

G. E. Bentley, Jr. and M. K. Nurmi. *Blake Bibliography*, 1964.

David Bindman. *William Blake: Catalogue of the Collection in the Fitzwilliam Museum*, Cambridge, 1970.

Laurence Binyon. *English Watercolours*, 1933.

Sir Anthony Blunt. *Art of William Blake*, 1959.

A. E. Bray. *Life of Thomas Stothard R.A.*, 2 vols., 1851.

British Museum. *Catalogue of Drawings by British Artists in the British Museum*, by Laurence Binyon, 4 vols., 1898–1907.

———. *Catalogue of British Drawings, vol. I: XVI and XVII centuries*, by Edward Croft-Murray and Paul Hulton, 1960.

Joseph Burke and Colin Caldwell. *Hogarth, the Complete Engravings*, 1968.

Adrian Bury. *Richard Wilson*, 1947.

Arthur B. Chamberlain. *George Romney*, 1910.

Sir Kenneth Clark. Introduction to *Catalogue of John Ruskin Exhibition*, Arts Council, 1960.

Rotha Mary Clay. *Julius Caesar Ibbetson*, 1948.

Derek Clifford. *Watercolours of the Norwich School*, 1965.

H. M. Colvin. *A Dictionary of British Architects 1660–1840*, 1954.

W. G. Constable. *Canaletto*, 1962.

———. *Richard Wilson*, 1953.

A. C. Coxhead. *Thomas Stothard R.A.*, 1906.

Edward Croft-Murray. *Decorative Painting in England 1537–1837*, 1962.

Edward Dayes. *The Works of the late E. Dayes*, 1805.

Dictionary of National Biography, 1908, etc.

Austin Dobson. *Hogarth*, 1907.

A. Dubuisson and C. A. Hughes. *Richard Parkes Bonington, his Life and Work*, 1924.

L. G. Duke. Manuscript catalogue of L. G. Duke's Collection of English Drawings (in the care of his literary executors, Judy Egerton and Dudley Snelgrove).

Edward Edwards. *Anecdotes of Painters* (etc.), 1806.

Joan Evans. *John Ruskin*, 1954.

Bernard Falk. *Thomas Rowlandson*, 1949.

Joseph Farington. *The Farington Diary*, edited by J. Greig, 7 vols., 1923–27.

A. J. Finberg. *Turner's Watercolours at Farnley Hall*, 1915.

——. *Early English Watercolours by the Great Masters*, 1919.

——. *Turner in Venice*, 1930.

——. *The Life of J. M. W. Turner R.A.*, 1961.

Hilda Finberg. *Canaletto in England*, Walpole Society, vol. IX, 1921–22.

Brinsley Ford. *The Drawings of Richard Wilson*, 1951.

Julia Frankau. *John Raphael Smith*, 1902.

Alexander Gilchrist. *Life of William Blake*, 2 vols., 1880.

Thomas Girtin and David Loshak. *The Art of Thomas Girtin*, 1954.

C. Reginald Grundy. *James Ward R.A.*, 1909.

Martin Hardie. *William Turner of Oxford*, Old Watercolour Society's Club, vol. IX, 1932.

——. *David Roberts R.A.*, Old Watercolour Society's Club, vol. XXV, 1947.

——. *Watercolour Painting in Britain*, 3 vols., 1966–68.

Francis Hawcroft. *Catalogue of Exhibition of John Robert Cozens*, Whitworth Art Gallery and Victoria and Albert Museum, 1971.

John Hayes. *Catalogue of the Oil Paintings in the London Museum*, 1970.

——. *The Drawings of Thomas Gainsborough*, 1970.

William Hayley. *Life of George Romney*, 1809.

Francis Hayman. *Catalogue of Francis Hayman Exhibition*, with notes by Mary Crake, Kenwood, 1960.

Luke Herrmann. "William Turner of Oxford," *Connoisseur*, vol. CLXII, August 1966.

Arthur M. Hind. *Wenceslaus Hollar and his views of London and Windsor*, 1922.

Philip Hofer. *Edward Lear as a Landscape Draughtsman*, 1967.

Charles Holmes. *The Genius of J. M. W. Turner*, 1903.

J. L. Howgego. Introduction to *Catalogue of William Marlow Exhibition*, Guildhall Art Gallery, 1956.

——. Introduction to *Catalogue of Sir James Thornhill Exhibition*, Guildhall Art Gallery, 1958.

Thomas Jones. *Memoirs*, Walpole Society, vol. XXXII, 1951.

Geoffrey Keynes. *A Bibliography of William Blake*, 1921.

Lord Killanin. *Sir Godfrey Kneller and his times: 1646–1723*, 1948.

Sydney D. Kitson. *The Life of John Sell Cotman*, 1937.

Francis Klingender. *Art and the Industrial Revolution*, edited and revised by Sir Arthur Elton, 1968.

Miloš Kratochvíl. *Hollar's Journey on the Rhine*, 1965.

Sir William Lamb. *The Royal Academy*, 1951.

Basil S. Long. "Robert Hills," *Walker's Quarterly*, no. 3, 1923.

———. "John 'Warwick' Smith," *Walker's Quarterly*, no. 24, 1927.

Edgar de N. Mayhew. *Sketches by Thornhill in the Victoria and Albert Museum*, 1967.

Jonathan Mayne. *Thomas Girtin*, 1949.

Benedict Nicolson. Introduction to *Catalogue of John Hamilton Mortimer Exhibition*, Eastbourne and Kenwood, 1968.

W. Foxley Norris. *Dr. Thomas Monro*, Old Watercolour Society's Club, vol. II, 1924.

James Northcote. *Memoirs of Sir Joshua Reynolds*, 1813.

A. P. Oppé. *Francis Towne*, Walpole Society, vol. VIII, 1920.

———. *Thomas Rowlandson, His Drawings and Watercolours*, 1923.

———. *The Watercolours of Turner, Cox and De Wint*, 1925.

———. *The Drawings of Paul and Thomas Sandby . . . at Windsor Castle*, 1947.

———. *The Drawings of William Hogarth*, 1948.

———. *English Drawings . . . at Windsor Castle*, 1950.

———. *Alexander and John Robert Cozens*, 1952.

James Orange. *The Chater Collection, Pictures relating to China, Hongkong and Macao, 1685–1860*, 1924.

A. H. Palmer. *Life and Letters of Samuel Palmer*, 1892.

Constance-Ann Parker. *Mr. Stubbs the Horse-Painter*, 1971.

Gustav Parthey. *Wenzel Hollar, Beschreibendes Verzeichniss seiner Kupferstiche*, 1853.

Ronald Paulson. *Hogarth, His Life, Art and Times*, 2 vols., 1971.

Nikolaus Pevsner. *The Buildings of England: London*, vol. I, 1957.

S. Rowland Pierce. *Jonathan Skelton and his Watercolours*, Walpole Society, vol. XXXVI, 1960.

Nicolas Powell. *The Drawings of Fuseli*, 1951.

———. "Brown and the Women of Rome," *Signature*, new series, vol. 14, 1952.

S. T. Prideaux. *Aquatint Engraving*, 1909.

Robert Raines. *Marcellus Laroon*, 1969.

W. G. Rawlinson. *The Engraved Work of J. M. W. Turner*, 2 vols., 1908, 1913.

Brian Reade. Introduction to *Catalogue of Edward Lear Exhibition*, Arts Council, 1958.

Samuel Redgrave. *A Dictionary of Artists of the English School*, 1878.

Graham Reynolds. *Nicholas Hilliard and Isaac Oliver*, 1947.

———. "British Artists Abroad, I, Captain Cook's Draughtsmen," *Geographical Magazine*, vol. xix, no. 10, 1947.

———. *An Introduction to English Watercolour Painting*, 1950.

———. *English Portrait Miniatures*, 1952.

———. *Catalogue of the Constable Collection in the Victoria and Albert Museum*, 1961.

———. *Constable, the Natural Painter*, 1965.

———. *A Concise History of Watercolours*, 1971.

J. L. Roget. *History of the Old Watercolour Society*, 2 vols., 1891.

Sir John Rothenstein and Martin Butlin. *Turner*, 1964.

William Sandby. *Thomas and Paul Sandby*, 1892.

Alastair Smart. *The Life and Art of Allan Ramsay*, 1952.

James Smetham. *Letters*, edited by S. Smetham and W. Davies, 1891.

John Thomas Smith. *Nollekens and his Times*, 1949 ed.

S. C. K. Smith. *Copley Fielding*, Old Watercolour Society's Club, vol. iii, 1925.

Neil N. Solly. *Memoirs of the Life of David Cox*, 1875.

W. Shaw Sparrow. *British Sporting Artists*, 1922.

Hugh Stokes. "James Holland," *Walker's Quarterly*, no. 23, 1927.

A. T. Story. *John Linnell*, 1892.

Thomas Sutton. *The Daniells, Artists and Travellers*, 1954.

Basil Taylor. *Animal Painting in England*, 1955.

———. *Stubbs*, 1971.

Ulrich Thieme and Felix Becker. *Allgemeines Lexikon der Bildenden Künstler*, Leipzig, 1950 (reprint).

Victoria and Albert Museum, Catalogue of Watercolour Paintings, 1927.

Horace Walpole. *Anecdotes of Painting in England*, 1762–63.

Robert R. Wark. *Rowlandson's Drawings for a Tour in a Post Chaise*, 1964.

———. *Rowlandson's Drawings for the English Dance of Death*, 1966.

Ellis K. Waterhouse. *Reynolds*, 1941.

Mary Webster. *Francis Wheatley*, 1970.

W. T. Whitley. *Artists and their friends in England, 1700–99*, 1928.

———. *Art in England, 1800–20*, 1928; *Art in England, 1821–37*, 1937.

Iolo A. Williams. *Early English Watercolours*, 1952.

———. *John 'Warwick' Smith*, Old Watercolour Society's Club, vol. xxiv, 1946.

George C. Williamson. *John Downman A.R.A.*, 1907.

Andrew Wilton. "An Appreciation of William Pars," in Richard Chandler, *Travels in Asia Minor*, edited and abridged by Edith Clay, 1971.

John Woodward. *Tudor and Stuart Drawings*, 1951.

ABBREVIATIONS

A.R.A.   Associate of the Royal Academy

L.B.   Laurence Binyon, *Catalogue of Drawings by British Artists in the British Museum*, 1898–1907

Colnaghi, 1964–65, and Yale University Art Gallery, 1965
                      P. & D. Colnaghi & Co. Ltd., London, *English Drawings and Watercolours from the Collection of Mr. and Mrs. Paul Mellon*, 14 December 1964 to 22 January 1965; this exhibition was later shown at the Yale University Art Gallery, New Haven, April–June 1965

D. (in provenance)
                      MS. catalogue of L. G. Duke's collection of English drawings, at present held by his literary executors, Judy Egerton and Dudley Snelgrove

Lugt   Frits Lugt, *Marques de Collections*, Amsterdam 1921, *Supplément*, The Hague 1956

P.R.A.   President of the Royal Academy

R.A.   Royal Academy; Royal Academician

R.H.A.   Royal Hibernian Academy

Victoria, 1971   The Art Gallery of Greater Victoria, Canada, *British Watercolour Drawings in the Collection of Mr. and Mrs. Paul Mellon*, 1971

V.M.F.A., 1963   Virginia Museum of Fine Arts, Richmond, Virginia, *Painting in England 1700–1850: Collection of Mr. and Mrs. Paul Mellon*, 1963

Washington, 1962   National Gallery of Art, Washington, *English Drawings and Watercolors from the Collection of Mr. and Mrs. Paul Mellon*, February–March 1962

ENGLISH DRAWINGS AND WATERCOLORS 1550-1850

Jacques Le Moyne de Morgues (c.1533–1588)

Le Moyne was a native of Dieppe. He appears to have had the patronage of Charles IX of France before he went as official artist to Florida on a Huguenot expedition under the command of René de Laudonnière. In September 1565 the strongpoint established by the French, called Fort Caroline (near present-day Jacksonville) was attacked by Pedro Menéndez, the first Spanish governor of Florida, who massacred most of the colonists there. Laudonnière, Le Moyne, and others who had escaped reached a ship which was anchored in St. John's River, and got back to France at the beginning of 1566. Le Moyne either sent or took back to France with him graphic work which he later developed into his own account of the colony. He fled to England "for religion," probably as a result of the St. Bartholomew's Day Massacre of 1572, and was established in Blackfriars, London, some time before 1581. There he supported himself as an artist and published a series of woodcuts of plant and animal subjects after his own drawings entitled *La Clef des Champs*. Le Moyne died in 1588.

1 A YOUNG DAUGHTER OF THE PICTS

Watercolor and gouache on vellum. 10¼ x 7¼ inches (26 x 18.5 cm.)
Provenance: H. P. Kraus, New York, 1968.

Until this drawing came to light, there was only one documented miniature painting by Le Moyne known to exist, apart from some studies of plants, namely, that of *Laudonnière and King Athore* in the New York Public Library. Stylistic comparison has convinced Paul Hulton that the exhibited drawing is by the same hand.

The drawing is apparently the original for Plate III of the section on Picts and Ancient Britons which follows John White's illustrations of Virginia in Theodor de Bry's appendix to his *Admiranda narratio fida tamen, de . . . Virginiae*, Frankfurt, 1590. De Bry added representations of the Picts in his book to those of the people of Virginia to display what he considered to be the similarities between the earliest inhabitants of England and the natives of Virginia.

1

Isaac Oliver (c.1556–1617)

The date of Oliver's birth is not known: Vertue deduced the year to be c.1556, but some evidence suggests a date nearer 1565. He was born in Rouen, whence his father, a Huguenot goldsmith, fled with his family from religious persecution about 1568. Oliver learned the art of portrait painting in miniature from Nicholas Hilliard, and at first followed his master's technique so closely that his earlier miniatures are not easily distinguishable from his master's. A contemporary called him Hilliard's "well profiting scholler," and indeed his work soon began to rival his master's in popularity. By 1604, when Oliver was appointed "her Ma^tes [Anne of Denmark's] painter for the Art of Lymning," he was enjoying fashionable repute. He became a naturalized Englishman in 1606, although he had long been numbered by contemporary English writers on art as among "our countrymen." He married three times, his second wife being the sister of the painter Marcus Gheeraerts the younger. He died in 1617, having bequeathed "all my drawings already finished and unfinished and limned pictures, be they histories, stories or anything of limning whatsoever ... to my eldest son Peter, if he shall live and exercise that art or science which he and I now do."

Graham Reynolds stresses that while Hilliard was an unequivocally British painter, Oliver's work on the whole presents an unmistakably alien, Italo-Flemish appearance. His drawings (which inevitably take second place to his superb miniatures) particularly reflect the influence of Parmigianino, whose work he had studied at first hand on a visit to Venice in 1596. Many of his drawings were set-pieces on classical, allegorical, or religious themes, the most ambitious being *The Entombment* (British Museum, 1945—9-24-2); but Vertue describes Oliver's habit of carrying about with him a pocket-book "to sketch in with a silver pen," and to note "sketches and postures" *extempore*. His drawings on the whole are elegant rather than poetic, and often do not rise above pastiche; but at his best he is a lively and a graceful draughtsman.

2 LEDA AND THE SWAN
Pen and sepia wash, heightened with white. 6⅜ x 8⅜ inches (16.2 x 21.3 cm.), on an early mount.
Provenance: Sir Thomas Lawrence (Lugt 2445); T. E. Lowinsky (Lugt 2420a); Justin Lowinsky 1963.

Inigo Jones (1573–1652)

Jones was born in London on 15 July 1573, son of a cloth-worker. Nothing is known about his training, but the earliest reference describes him as "a picture maker"; he is said to have begun by painting landscapes, and one attributed to him is at Chatsworth. He is believed to have first visited Italy in 1601, and to have been invited thence to the court of Christian IV, King of Denmark, whose sister Anne, Queen of James I, gave him constant patronage after his return to England. Between 1604 and 1640 he designed scenery and costumes for a series of lavish and costly court masques; his designs for these have survived, and include some monochrome landscapes of a highly imaginative kind. From 1613 to 1614 he was in Italy, advising Lord Arundel and others on the collecting of works of art, nourishing his own admiration of Italian achievements (a sketchbook at Chatsworth contains his copies from Italian masters) and, in particular, studying the architecture of Palladio, whose drawings he himself collected. On his return neither the court masques nor his notorious wrangles with Ben Jonson over them seriously distracted him from the most substantial work of his life: architecture. He was appointed Surveyor of the King's Works in 1615, and the next year began work on the Queen's House at Greenwich, upon a design whose classicism was to be a timely leaven in the overelaborate lump of Jacobean taste. In a series of churches and houses (notably the Banqueting House in Whitehall and St. Paul's Church, Covent Garden) he established the English Palladian style, which was to be a ruling influence. Charles I having continued the royal patronage, Jones repaid him not only by embellishing his capital but also with valuable advice on enriching the royal art collection. An ardent Royalist, Jones suffered a fine and a brief imprisonment during the Civil War; he was pardoned, but thereafter his health deteriorated, and he died at Somerset House in June 1652.

3 HEAD OF A BOY

Pen and sepia ink. 5⅝ x 5½ inches (14.3 x 14 cm.)

Inscribed: Verso *Inigo Jones,* in ink, in an old hand.

Provenance: Lord Milford; Erasmus Philipps; Sir John Philipps; H. Calmann 1943; T. E. Lowinsky (Lugt 2420a); Justin Lowinsky 1963.

Wenceslaus Hollar (1607–1677)

Hollar was born in Prague in 1607, within a year of the birth of Rembrandt. He was the son of Jan Hollar, an official in the service of Rudolf II. According to John Aubrey, who was personally acquainted with the artist and was his earliest biographer, Hollar's father suffered as a result of his adherence to Frederick of the Palatinate, the unfortunate Winter King of Bohemia. Aubrey also speaks in his *Brief Lives* of Hollar's delight as a boy in "draweing of Mapps." In 1627 Hollar left Prague and spent some two years apprenticed to Matthäus Merian the Elder, the topographical etcher in Frankfurt. In 1628 he moved to Strasbourg by way of Stuttgart. In 1629 he embarked on a journey along the Rhine and settled in Cologne. He visited Holland in 1634 and 1635. In the spring of 1636 he met the famous diplomatist and collector, the Earl of Arundel, who was traveling on an embassy to the Imperial Court. The Earl engaged Hollar to accompany his suite as draughtsman. By the end of the year Arundel was back in England, and Hollar returned with him.

For the next few years Hollar, now residing at Arundel House, was busy etching plates after drawings and other works of art in the Earl's collection, as well as executing a number of his London Views. About 1639 he was appointed teacher of drawing in the Royal Household and shortly thereafter he was attached to the service of the Duke of York as "serviteur domestique." In 1641 Hollar married Mrs. Tracy, Lady-in-Waiting to the Countess of Arundel. They had a daughter, whom Aubrey describes as "one of the greatest beauties I have seen," and a son who died of the plague at the age of seventeen. At the commencement of the Civil War, the Earl of Arundel went into exile at Antwerp. During the war Hollar served with his fellow-artists Inigo Jones and William Faithorne under the Marquis of Winchester. Hollar was apparently taken prisoner in 1644 before the siege of Basing House by the Parliamentarians, but managed to escape to Antwerp, where he sought out his patron. The Earl of Arundel died in 1646, and Hollar returned to England in 1652, possibly at the invitation of Elias Ashmole, Sir William Dugdale, or John Aubrey. He was arrested on his arrival because of his earlier Royalist connections but was released at Dugdale's request. He lodged at the houses of various printsellers, working for small pay. His fortunes did not greatly improve with the Restoration. He married again in 1665. In 1669 he was sent with Lord Henry Howard's expedition to Tangiers (part of Catherine of Braganza's dowry on her marriage to Charles II) to make drawings of the town and fortifications. On the return journey their ship narrowly escaped capture by Algerian pirates. During his last years Hollar did a great deal of work producing plates for booksellers. The vast number of plates from his hand points not only to his industry but also to the fact that he was hard pressed to make a living. He was clearly no man of business: instead of making a fixed charge for the plates, he reckoned by an hourglass, and, as his friend the amateur and etcher Francis Place related, "if anybody came in, and kept him from his business, he always laid the hourglass on one side, till they were gone."

Hollar died indigent and a Catholic at the age of 70, and was buried at St. Margaret's, Westminster, on 28 March 1677.

4 STUDY FOR THE "LONG BIRD'S-EYE VIEW OF LONDON FROM BANKSIDE, 1647"

Pen and ink over pencil. 5 x 12⅛ inches (12.7 x 30.8 cm.), top left corner cut.

Inscribed: ~~East Part~~ [sic] *West Part o* [sic] *Southwarke toward Westminster* in ink, top center.

Provenance: Patrick Allan Fraser (sold Sotheby's 10 June 1931); Iolo A. Williams; Colnaghi 1964.

Literature: "Hollar: A discovery of Iolo A. Williams," *Connoisseur*, November 1933, pp. 309–13; Franz Sprinzels, *Hollar Handzeichnungen*, Vienna, 1938; I. A. Shapiro, "An Original Drawing of the Globe Theatre," *Shakespeare Survey*, 2, 1949.

Exhibited: Graves Art Gallery, Sheffield, *Early English Water-colours from the Collection of Iolo A. Williams*, 1952, no. 2(a).

This drawing and a companion subject looking east, also from the Iolo Williams collection (exhibited Colnaghi's, 1964, no. 2, pl. 11), are studies for the *Long Bird's-Eye View of London from Bankside, 1647*. The subject was etched on six plates and according to Hollar's signature was made in Antwerp in 1647. He used the drawing exhibited here, with minor variations, for the three left-hand plates, and the view toward the east for the right-hand two plates. In both drawings details on the north bank are only roughly described in pencil, whereas the topography is complete in the etching. A. M. Hind suggests that Hollar made these studies, initially in pencil and later outlined in ink in his own hand, from the tower of St. Mary Overy's (St. Saviour's, Southwark), some time during his stay in England which began with his arrival with Lord Arundel at the end of 1636 and lasted until his departure for Antwerp in 1644.

Significant buildings portrayed include Old St. Paul's, seen in rough pencil outline in the upper right corner; the Globe Theatre (not Shakespeare's theatre but one built on the same site very shortly after the former's destruction by fire in 1613) can be seen in the middle distance on the banks of the Thames, and to the left of it a similar building used for the sport of bear-baiting.

5 VIEW OF STEIERECK ON THE DANUBE
Pen and bistre with blue wash. 3$\frac{15}{16}$ x 9¼ inches (10 x 23.5 cm.)
Inscribed: *Steiereck* top center, and *Danubius Fluvius* on the river.
Provenance: George Salting; Sir Harry Baldwin; John Baskett 1970.

Steiereck is situated a few miles east of Linz on the Danube. Hollar would have passed it in 1636 with Lord Arundel and his suite en route by river for Vienna to execute the latter's confidential mission for Charles I of England. The drawings Hollar made during this journey were presumably intended, although in fact they were not used, to act as illustrations in the form of engravings to the journal kept by William Crowe, Lord Arundel's secretary, which was published in 1637 after their return to England.

William Faithorne (1616?-1691)

Faithorne was born in London. He was apprenticed to a goldsmith, but in a short time was working under master engravers. Sir Robert Peake, painter to Charles I and printseller, had Faithorne not only as a pupil, but as a Royalist supporter under his command at the siege of Basing House in 1645. After the surrender to Cromwell's troops, Faithorne was imprisoned in Aldersgate in London, where he was permitted to continue his engraving, even, when iconography surmounted their principles, engraving portraits of Cromwell and some of his leaders. After his release from prison he was exiled to Paris, not returning to London until 1650 to set up business in a printshop. After the Restoration he prospered through royal patronage and worked in a coterie of highly skilled artists and notables, Hollar, Place, Pepys, and Aubrey among them. Faithorne was a victim of lingering consumption; he died in May 1691 and was buried on the 13th day of that month at Blackfriars, London.

6 PORTRAIT OF A LADY
Colored chalks. 9½ x 8⅛ inches (24.3 x 20.8 cm.)
Provenance: L. G. Duke (D.3875), sold Sotheby's 22 October 1970, lot 71; John Baskett 1970.

L. G. Duke notes that the handling corresponds closely with Faithorne's drawing of Sir Edmund King in the British Museum (1847–3-26-5).

Thomas Wyck (c. 1616 – 1677)

Thomas Wyck was born at Beverwyck near Haarlem about 1616. He became a pupil of Pieter van Laer, presumably at some time during the latter's stay in Italy between 1626 and 1639. Back in Holland, Wyck became a member of the Haarlem Guild in 1642. He painted Italianate landscapes with courtyards, Roman buildings, and ruins pervaded by the warm Mediterranean sunlight; he also specialized in the then fashionable themes of philosophers, and alchemists brewing their concoctions in dingy interiors.

In 1663, for reasons that are not known, Wyck traveled to England. Vertue (who mistakenly puts Wyck's arrival in England between 1667 and 1668) states that "Lord Burlington had a long prospect (by Wyck) of London and the Thames, taken from Southwark, before the Fire"; he adds that "Mr. Wyck painted the View of the fire of the City of London several times very well." Vertue also writes that Jan van der Vaart "some time learnt of Old Mr. Wyke, in England." As van der Vaart did not arrive in England until 1674, one is led to presume that Wyck was still resident in England at that time. This information is corroborated by the fact that Thomas Wyck's son Jan appeared before the Court of the Painter-Stainers on 17 June 1674 to promise to pay his father's "quarterage." Three years later Wyck had returned to Haarlem, where he died; he was buried on 19 August 1677.

7 VIEW OF THE WATERHOUSE AND OLD ST. PAUL'S, LONDON
Black lead and gray wash. 9 x 13½ inches (22.7 x 34.2 cm.)
Provenance: Horace Walpole; Dr. H. Wellesley; Gardner; Major Sir Edward Feetham Coates; The Lady Celia Milnes Coates, sold Christie's 23 November 1971, lot 137; John Baskett 1971.

This drawing, which was clearly executed on the spot, must have been made very shortly after Wyck's arrival in 1663, as the Waterhouse was demolished in 1664, and Old St. Paul's was burned down two years later in the Great Fire.

Francis Barlow (1626? – 1704)

The date and place of Barlow's birth are both uncertain, although tradition has it that he was born in 1626 in Lincolnshire. According to George Vertue he was apprenticed to "Shepherd, a Face Painter": possibly William Sheppard, who painted a portrait of Thomas Killigrew in 1650. Barlow appears to have turned his attention at an early date to drawing and painting animals and birds, as Vertue describes "his Genious leading him wholly to drawing of Fowl, Fish and Beasts, wherein he arrived to that Perfection, that had his Colouring and Pencilling been as good as his Draught, which was most exact, he might easily have excell'd all that went before him in that kind of Painting."

Barlow secured the support and patronage of several eminent men including General Monck, later first Duke of Albemarle, Sir Francis Prujean, physician to Queen Catherine, and John Hervey, later first Earl of Bristol. He failed to obtain the diarist John Evelyn's patronage, despite dedicating an engraving of Titian's *Venus* to him in 1656. Evelyn, however, wrote of him in that year as "the famous painter of Fowle, Beasts and Birds." Vertue reported that he made some ceiling designs of birds for country houses. As a painter he belongs to that circle of mainly Dutch artists at work in England painting animal subjects, and including Hondius, Griffier, Thomas and Jan Wyck, Hondecoeter, Bogdany, and Casteels.

Barlow made a large number of drawings for book illustration, sometimes etching them himself. The most famous of these are his illustrations to Aesop's *Fables*, many of the designs for which are preserved in the British Museum. A large number of Barlow's animal and bird drawings were engraved by his contemporary, Francis Place. Place, the country-gentleman artist, must have thought highly of Barlow's work for he declined an invitation to resell a group sent to him by the publisher Tempest: "I have charged Barlow's drawings in it," Tempest writes in 1693 concerning Place's account; "when you have done wth them I think I have a chapman will give me five shillings a peece for them wch is Mr Smith who would have bought them before."

Vertue states that "notwithstanding all Mr. Barlow's Excellency in his way, and tho' he had the good Fortune to have a considerable Sum of Money left him by a Friend, he died poor in the year 1702." Vertue is wrong as to the date, for Barlow is now known to have been buried in St. Margaret's, Westminster, on 11 August 1704.

8 HARE HUNTING

Pen and brown ink with gray wash. 6⅞ x 9⅞ inches (17.5 x 25 cm.)

Provenance: L. G. Duke (D.125); Colnaghi 1961.

Literature: W. Shaw Sparrow, "British Art at the Royal Academy," *The Field*, 30 December 1933 (ill.); Rose Macaulay, *Life among the English*, 1942, p. 27 (ill.); John Woodward, *Tudor and Stuart Drawings*, 1951, p. 48; Whinney and Millar, *English Art 1625–1714*, 1957, p. 279, pl. 78b.

Exhibited: Royal Academy, *British Art*, 1934, no. 538; 39 Grosvenor Square, London, *British Country Life*, 1937, no. 462; Bristol City Art Gallery, *Stuart Drawings*, 1952, no. 4; Royal Academy, *Old Master Drawings*, 1953, no. 441; Royal Academy, *The Age of Charles II*, 1960–61, no. 506; National Gallery, Washington, 1962, no. 2 (ill.); V.M. F.A., Richmond, 1963, no. 389; Colnaghi, 1964–65, and Yale University Art Gallery, 1965, no. 3 (ill.).

Engraved: In mezzotint by J. Collins.

Sir Godfrey Kneller (1646 or 1649–1723)

Kneller was born at Lübeck, son of a surveyor and portrait painter. He studied at Leyden intending a military career, but his main urge was to paint, and his father sent him to study at Amsterdam under Ferdinand Bol; he also had some lessons from Rembrandt. In 1672 he was studying historical painting in Italy, and, at that time, developed his gift for painting portraits. After spending some time in Hamburg, he arrived in London in 1675 to lodge with Jonathan Banks, a wealthy merchant. Kneller painted portraits of the Banks family, and these were seen by many people of influence. His commissions mounted and his reputation soon reached the court, his first portrait of Charles II being painted in 1678. Kneller continued to paint royal likenesses through three reigns, and in 1691 was honored with a knighthood, and created a baronet in 1715. Requests for portraits came in such quantity that Kneller employed a group of assistants to paint draperies and backgrounds, confining himself to the head and sometimes the hands of the sitters.

Kneller was a man of handsome features and good bearing, and blessed with good health throughout his life. He bought an estate at Whitton, Middlesex, and the house as it now stands, although much altered, is used as the School for Military Music. Kneller died at Whitton on 19 October 1723.

9 PORTRAIT OF JOHN LOCKE, THE PHILOSOPHER
Red chalk on buff paper, heightened with white. 12⅛ x 8⅞ inches (30.8 x 22 cm.)
Provenance: Robinson Bros. 1961.

Jonathan Richardson I (1665–1745)

Richardson was a pupil of the painter John Riley (1646–1691). He married Riley's niece and is said to have inherited a large number of his master's drawings. Richardson senior is better known as a collector than as an artist. He etched portraits of the collectors Lord Somers and Richard Mead, and of Bolingbroke and Pope, as well as writing books on art and art theory. Walpole describes him as "a formal man, with a slow but loud and sonorous voice, and, in truth, with some affectation in his manner." Matthew Prior goes further, suggesting that Richardson call a projected book on art "The History of Myself, My Son Jonathan, with a Word or Two about Raphael and Michelangelo by the Way." Such comments would seem to fit the rather humorless features seen in the countless self-portraits which have come down to us, most of which were made toward the end of his life.

As a collector, Richardson senior must have possessed a remarkable eye, and his collector's mark on a drawing is a pointer to quality. Richardson provided the expert advice when Lord Somers acquired through Talman the sixteen volumes containing over 2,500 drawings from the nephew of Monsignore Marchetti, Bishop of Arezzo, a collection chosen for the Bishop by Padre Resta. Richardson is supposed to have obtained drawings for himself direct from Resta before the sale to Lord Somers, and it is also said that he imitated Padre Resta's mounts for drawings from his own collection. Richardson arranged the collections of the Duke of Devonshire and of the Earl of Pembroke, and acquired some fine drawings for them. After his death on 28 May 1745, the sale of his own collection comprised 4,749 drawings and, according to Walpole, there were yet more that were not dispersed until his son's sale in 1772.

10 HEAD OF A YOUNG MAN WITH LONG HAIR

Red and black chalk. 12¼ x 10⅜ inches (31.2 x 26.5 cm.)

Inscribed: Verso in ink, in an early hand, *Drawing by Richardson.*

Provenance: Iolo A. Williams; Colnaghi 1964.

Another version of this drawing, similar in medium and paper, 13¾ x 11 inches, is in the Witt Collection, Courtauld Institute (no. 2829). It was shown in the *Sir Godfrey Kneller* exhibition at the National Portrait Gallery (cat. no. 49) in 1971, there attributed to Kneller.

Sir James Thornhill (1675 or 1676–1734)

Thornhill was born at Woolland in Dorset on 25 July 1675 or 1676, the son of Walter Thornhill of Wareham. He was apprenticed in 1689 to the painter Thomas Highmore, in whose studio he may have continued to work as assistant after serving his apprenticeship. Thornhill's style was considerably influenced by that of the decorative painters Verrio and Laguerre; he may have worked with Verrio, but Laguerre's style, with its predominantly French flavor, was formative in his development. An additional influence was the Venetian style of painters such as Ricci and Pellegrini who came to England in the 1720's.

Thornhill became a director of Kneller's Academy in 1711, and its governor in 1716. He was appointed History Painter in Ordinary to the King in 1718; in 1720 he succeeded Highmore as Sergeant Painter and became Master of the Painter-Stainers' Company, and in the same year became the first British artist to receive the honor of knighthood. He was elected Member of Parliament for Weymouth in 1722, and Fellow of the Royal Society in 1723. He resigned his post of Sergeant Painter in 1732. He died at Thornhill Park in Dorset on 13 May 1734.

Thornhill's most important commission, and the one upon which his fame rests, is the decoration of the Painted Hall at Greenwich from 1707. Apart from the (now destroyed) Chapel and Hall at Windsor Castle, it is the richest and most successful baroque painted room in England. Other important commissions were Chatsworth and Hampton Court (both c.1702, early in his career), the dome of St. Paul's Cathedral from 1714, and a characteristic surviving domestic work, the staircase at Hanbury Hall, c.1710. As a painter Thornhill was uneven. His oil sketches vary widely in quality. His preliminary drawings are, however, greatly prized as brilliant studies pregnant with ideas.

11 DESIGN FOR CEILING, WALLS, AND STAIRCASE

Pen, ink, and brown wash. 15¼ x 19⅝ inches (38.5 x 50 cm.)

Inscribed: On the ceiling *Gratitude, ye Principal figure, crowned by Peace, and order, wch Providence particularly presides. Industry, leaning on a bee hive, attended by Plenty, and holding a Plan or upright of Fort St. George. Fame, sounding ye Praise of Gratitude and Industry*; and, on the walls *Sylla's Triumph, is followed by ye Citizens etc. wth loud acclamations, in that he had redeemed them from Slavery. Sylla gratefully offers ye 10th of all his Spoyls to Hercules etc. The Roman People, Ladys etc serries [?] to adorn . . . Sylla.*

Provenance: Colnaghi 1970.

This design is inscribed for, or signed by, Thomas Pitt (1653–1726), familiarly known as "Diamond Pitt." Pitt returned from India and settled in England in 1710, so it might be expected that he embarked upon building works in the ensuing five to ten years. In 1715 he became a Commissioner for Building New Churches, an appointment that would have brought him into contact with Thornhill and his circle; moreover he was, like Thornhill, a native of Dorset. The Pitt Account Book (Chancery Masters Exhibits, Public Record Office) records that Pitt employed John James to design a house in London and for work at Swallowfield Park in Berkshire. He also owned Mawarden Court, Stratford, Essex, and the old family seat, The Down, near Blandford. It is possible that Thornhill's staircase design was proposed for the London house, but it is more likely to have been for Swallowfield, Pitt's favorite residence. Swallowfield had been built by William Talman for Lord Clarendon in 1689. Its interior was, however, extensively altered in 1820 when the old staircase was eliminated. Stylistically Thornhill's design groups itself with Hanbury Hall of c.1710.

John Wootton (c.1678–1765)

Wootton was born about 1678. He studied painting under Jan Wyck, a master of battle and hunting scenes, and later worked in the studio of the landscape painter Siberechts. Assistance from one of his patrons, the third Duke of Beaufort, enabled him to study in Rome. The influences which shaped his style were thus predominantly Italian and Flemish; but his preferred subject-matter was essentially English: "horses and dogs," in Walpole's words, "which he both drew and coloured with consummate skill, fire and truth." Wootton made his name painting racehorses at Newmarket. He soon had so many commissions that he was able to charge high prices, and to establish himself in a fine studio in Cavendish Square. The King, grumbling over dinner at Newmarket that Mr. Wootton made him pay twenty guineas for a half-length picture of a horse, found many of his noblemen eager to pay Wootton's prices for portraits of their horses and hounds, their hunts, and equestrian portraits of themselves. Much of Wootton's work was on a large scale, and many of his paintings remain in the country houses for which they were made, such as Althorp, Longleat, and Welbeck. Wootton also painted battle scenes and, later in life, landscape in the manner of Claude and Poussin. An air of ceremony attends most of Wootton's compositions, expressed in this drawing by the hunting horn which will shortly summon the resting hounds to their role. Wootton worked mainly in oils; his drawings are rare. He died at his London house in January 1765.

12 HOUNDS IN A LANDSCAPE
Pen and brown ink over black chalk with gray wash. 8¾ x 8 inches (22.4 x 20.3 cm.)
Inscribed: *Mr. Wooton* on border of the early mount.
Provenance: John Baskett 1970.

The drawing bears some relation to Wootton's painting *Althorp Hounds and the Magpie,* in the collection of Earl Spencer.

Marcellus Laroon II (1679–1772)

Laroon was born on 2 April 1679, the second of the three sons of Marcellus Laroon, an artist of Dutch-French ancestry who had come to England at an early age, and married an English-woman. The father, who is sometimes called "Old Laroon," taught Marcellus painting and drawing and employed a French music master. Unable to provide an education which embraced anything approaching the Grand Tour, "Old Laroon" nevertheless saw to it that Marcellus had opportunity to travel, by arranging for him to go in 1697 as page in the suite of one of the plenipotentiaries to the Congress of Ryswick at The Hague, and later to go on to Venice in the same role with the fourth Earl of Manchester. Marcellus would have found the opportunity in Venice of attending the opera and the *Commedia dell'Arte* as well as looking at pictures.

Returning to England in 1698 Marcellus quarreled with his father and took employment at Drury Lane Theatre as a singer. He pursued this career for some eight years, and then in 1707 got himself attached to the first Regiment of Foot Guards, declaring that he was "resolved to carry arms," presumably to distinguish the purpose of his career from the sort of social diversion that Boswell sought in his efforts to join the army. Marcellus Laroon, or "Captain Laroon" as he came to be known to distinguish him from his father, was active in Flanders and Spain and saw intermittent service with the army until his retirement in 1732.

Most of what is known about Marcellus Laroon has been assembled by Dr. Robert Raines from John Thomas Smith's publication of Laroon's autobiographical manuscripts in *Nollekens and his Times* and from Vertue's scattered notes. Unfortunately the autobiographical passage ends with Laroon's departure from the army at the age of 53, leaving another forty years virtually unrecorded. It would appear, however, that Laroon, being a rather extroverted personality of lively disposition, continued to enjoy life in and around Covent Garden, maintaining his interest in the theatre, music, and the arts. He made drawings to give to friends, played the violin and 'cello, and engaged in a little desultory picture-dealing. He retained his facility for drawing right up to the end of his life, dying at Oxford on 1 June 1772 at the age of 93.

13 LOVERS IN A GLADE

Pencil. Paper 14⅜ x 11¼ inches (36.5 x 28 cm.); subject 13½ x 10⅜ inches (34.4 x 26.4 cm.)

Inscribed: M. L. Fe. *1759* in pencil lower right.
Provenance: Basil Taylor; John Baskett 1968.
Literature: Robert Raines, *Marcellus Laroon*, 1969, p. 134, no. 61, pl. 50.
Exhibited: Tate Gallery, *Marcellus Laroon*, 1967, no. 46.

The gestures of the figures and the flat backdrop appearance of the trees behind the bank on which the lovers are seated suggest that this drawing might be a scene from a theatrical production.

Bernard Lens III (1682–1740)

The name Bernard Lens was borne by four successive generations of artists. Similarity in their style (especially in topographical monochromes) and overlap in their dates of working, have inevitably led to confusion in attribution. Iolo Williams, in his *Early English Watercolours*, achieved a satisfactory division of the dates and activities of the Lens family.

Bernard Lens III was born in London; his father was a mezzotint engraver and drawing-master. He studied at Kneller's Academy of Painting, although he was almost 30 when it opened in 1711. He became one of the principal miniature painters of the time, and enjoyed the patronage of two kings, George I and George II. He was equally successful as a drawing-master, his distinguished pupils including the royal children, the Duchess of Portland, Mrs. Delany, and Horace Walpole. In one of his manuals he instructs the young practitioner to "divide a figure into ten Faces," and gives a table of proportions, such as "From the navel to the Privities, one Face," and "Your longest toe is the length of your nose."

Lens was a versatile craftsman, working also in mezzotint, engraving, and enamel. He died in Knightsbridge, London, on 30 December 1740.

14 FIGURES ON THE BANK OF THE LONG WATER, HAMPTON COURT PALACE

Pen and gray wash. 8⅝ x 12¾ inches (22 x 32.6 cm.)
Provenance: Iolo A. Williams; Colnaghi 1964.

Numerous drawings of views in and around London were made in gray monochrome by members of the Lens family, copying one another. Certain drawings, such as the above, could be considered to be early fashion plates. Two albums by Bernard Lens, one in the Victoria and Albert Museum and the other at Windsor, show women's headdress for the years 1725 and 1727.

Antonio Canaletto (1697–1768)

Antonio Canal, commonly called Canaletto, was born in Venice in 1697. His reputation rests chiefly on his famous Venetian views, but he came to England in 1746 and remained, with one short interval, until 1754 or 1755. It seems evident that Canaletto made his visit because the War of the Austrian Succession had depressed his business in Venice, for Englishmen were no longer able to make the Grand Tour. Canaletto's first patron in England was the Duke of Richmond, for whom he painted, shortly after his arrival, the beautiful views of *The Thames from Richmond House* and *Whitehall from Richmond House*. Among his other patrons during his residence in England were Sir Hugh Smithson, Bart., afterwards first Duke of Northumberland, the Duke of Beaufort, and Lord Brooke, afterwards Earl of Warwick; and his subjects encompassed a number of views of London and its environs, and scenes taken from visits to his patrons' seats at Alnwick and Warwick Castles.

By 1756 Canaletto was back in Venice where, with all his old enthusiasm though now nearly sixty years old, he resumed painting views of his beloved city. He died there on 20 April 1768.

15 VIEW ON THE THAMES FROM YORK STAIRS SHOWING WESTMINSTER BRIDGE

Pen, sepia ink, and gray wash. 15¼ x 28¼ inches (38.7 x 71.7 cm.)

Provenance: Robert Prioleau Roupell, sold Christie's, 12 July 1887; J. P. Heseltine; M. Bernard; Colnaghi 1961.

Literature: J. Beresford Chancellor, *Eighteenth Century London*, 1920, p. 154; Hilda Finberg, *A Catalogue Raisonné of Canaletto's English Views*, Walpole Society, 1921, vol. IX, p. 69, pl. xxxiii; W. G. Constable, *Canaletto*, 1962, p. 529, no. 747.

Exhibited: Whitechapel, St. Jude's, 1888, no. 176; New Gallery, *Venetian Art*, 1894–95, no. 322; Whitechapel Art Gallery, 1911, no. 11; Burlington Fine Arts Club, *Early Drawings and Pictures of London*, 1919, no. 11; Grosvenor Gallery, 1935; Royal Academy, *European Masters of the Eighteenth Century*, 1954, no. 582; Guildhall Art Gallery, *Canaletto in England*, 1959, no. 53; V.M.F.A., Richmond, 1963, no. 477; Colnaghi, 1964–65, and Yale University Art Gallery, 1965, no. 7 (ill.).

The construction of Westminster Bridge was started in 1737 and continued for over a decade under the supervision of the Swiss architect Charles Labelye. It was apparently completed in 1748, when one of the piers began to subside out of line. Another drawing by Canaletto at Windsor Castle shows workmen removing stonework off the sinking pier in 1749. It is curious that the *View from York Stairs*, which must date from after Canaletto's arrival in England in 1746, shows the bridge less than half completed.

There is a clumsy copy in the British Museum which Hadeln (*Canaletto Drawings*, 1929, p. 12) wrongly refers to as an original.

16 OLD WALTON BRIDGE SEEN FROM THE MIDDLESEX SHORE

Pen, ink, and gray wash. 13 x 32 inches (33 x 81.2 cm.)

Inscribed: *Disegnato da me Antonio Canal detto Canaleto* [sic] *appresso il mio Quadro Dippinto in Londra 1755 / per il Signore Cavaliere Dicker* at center below the drawing.

Provenance: Fauchier-Magnan; Agnew 1959.

Literature: W. G. Constable, *Canaletto*, 1962, vol. II, no. 755 and vol. I, pl. 142.

Exhibited: Royal Academy, *Drawings by Old Masters*, 1953, no. 180.

The painting from which Canaletto took this drawing is also in the Mellon collection. An engraving of the view by A. Walker is dedicated to Samuel Dicker "at whose sole Charge the said Bridge was Erected in the year 1750". Dicker, whose house is among trees on the left of the drawing, was Member of Parliament for Portsmouth and died in 1760.

William Hogarth (1697–1764)

Hogarth was born in London on 10 November 1697, son of a schoolmaster from Westmorland. He was apprenticed to a silversmith, Ellis Gamble, until he was nearly twenty, then changed from this branch of engraving to making copperplates of shop bills, book illustrations, and bookplates. In his spare time he studied at Cheron and Vanderbank's academy in St. Martin's Lane, but essentially he taught himself painting. He started business on his own in 1720, and while he depended on making plates for clients and booksellers, he also produced searching satires projected against people and events which he held in contempt. He frequently drew from the life at Sir James Thornhill's academy and became a friend of the Thornhill family. In 1729 he made a clandestine marriage with Jane Thornhill with, it is said, Lady Thornhill's connivance. The estrangement with Thornhill over this was short-lived and the families remained on close terms until he died in 1734. By 1731, Hogarth had painted the first of his moral narratives, six canvases depicting *A Harlot's Progress*. These he engraved and published himself within a few months of painting them, and so successful was their appeal that Hogarth had 1,200 subscribers of, according to Vertue, "persons of all ranks and conditions from the greatest quality to the meanest." The pictures embodied the backcloths of scenes in his daily life, and personalities and types that conformed to the low standards which he deplored. His wish was, to use his own words, "to compose pictures on canvass, similar to representations on the stage" and "to treat my subjects as a dramatic writer . . . who by means of certain actions are to exhibit a *dumb show*." Hogarth's other inventions, far from dumb, came to life in *The Rake's Progress*, 1735, *Marriage à la Mode*, 1745, and *Industry and Idleness*, 1747.

An event of light-heartedness that must have been a relief from his work on the *Harlot* came two months after publication. A spontaneous junket from Billingsgate to Rochester and the coast of Kent, lasting five days, was made by Hogarth and four friends. This "Peregrination," recorded in diary form illustrated with seven drawings by Hogarth and two by Samuel Scott, one of the companions, is preserved in the British Museum together with a copy of it by Rowlandson. Ebenezer Forrest, the appointed "historian" of the five, kept an account which was later written up in lengthy verse by Canon Gostling, an antiquary of Canterbury, the two versions showing how much the adventure was enjoyed with the boisterous vulgarity of the time.

From 1733 onwards, Hogarth lived and worked at the "Golden Head," Leicester Fields, and shortly afterwards founded an academy in St. Martin's Lane. His action against the blatant plagiarism of his plates was responsible for an Act of Parliament that protected engravers from this iniquitous practice.

Hogarth's book, *Analysis of Beauty*, intending to fix the "fluctuating Ideas of Taste," was praised by some, but provided his rivals and enemies with endless material for ridicule and caricature. He rather anticipated this when he wrote in an epigram, "All he's gained by the *pencil*, he'll *lose* by the pen." Appreciation for his painting was unaffected, however, and he succeeded Thornhill as Sergeant Painter to George II and held the appointment under George III. He died on 26 October 1764 and was buried at Chiswick. A tomb was erected to him there in 1771 with an epitaph by his friend David Garrick, the famous actor, two lines of which seem to sum up Hogarth's aspirations,

> Whose *pictur'd morals* charm the Mind
> And through the Eye correct the Heart.

17 HEADING TO THE SUBSCRIPTION ROLL FOR THE FOUNDLING HOSPITAL, 1739

Pen, ink, and wash. 4⅜ x 8⅜ inches (11.2 x 21.2 cm.)

Provenance: H. P. Standly; Lady Capel Cure; Maas Gallery 1965.

Literature: A. P. Oppé, *Drawings of William Hogarth*, 1948, no. 66; R. H. Nichols and F. A. Wray, *History of the Foundling Hospital*, 1935, pp. 249, 278; Austin Dobson, *Hogarth*, 1907, p. 245.

Engraved: F. M. La Cave.

The Foundling Hospital was granted a charter in 1739 on the petition of Captain Thomas Coram, philanthropist and merchant. Its aim was to provide for the "maintenance and education of exposed and deserted young children" and to prevent their murder or abandonment in the streets. Children were admitted freely at first, but as applications overwhelmed the administration, a system of ballot was adopted. Captain Coram's tangible example of charity led the government in 1756 to appoint local receiving places for children throughout the country. At Hogarth's instigation, principal artists of the time, including Highmore, Hayman, Wilson, and Gainsborough, presented their paintings to the hospital as an act of charity. Intended or not, this provided the first venue in London for these painters to exhibit collectively to a wide public work which had hitherto been available only in their own studios.

18 THE INDUSTRIOUS 'PRENTICE OUT OF HIS TIME AND MARRIED TO HIS MASTER'S DAUGHTER

Pencil and black ink, marked for squaring, partly incised. Verso, pink preparation for transfer to plate. Subject 8¼ x 11⅜ inches (21 x 29 cm.), paper 9⅞ x 12⅞ inches (25.1 x 32.6 cm.)

Provenance: The Marquess of Exeter; Edward Speelman 1962.

Literature: A. P. Oppé, *Drawings of William Hogarth*, 1948, no. 49; J. Burke and C. Caldwell, *Hogarth, The Complete Engravings*, 1968, pl. 208*.

Engraved: By Hogarth, pl. vi of the series.

Exhibited: V.M.F.A., Richmond, 1963, no. 393.

A more finished drawing for this subject is in the British Museum (1896–7-10-14) in which the wheelbarrow has been replaced by a child and a dog, and the woman receiving alms is carrying only one child in her arms.

19 THE INDUSTRIOUS 'PRENTICE MARRIED AND FURNISHING HIS HOUSE

Brown ink and gray wash. Subject 8¼ x 11⅜ inches (21 x 29 cm.), paper 9⅞ x 13⅛ inches (25.1 x 33.5 cm.). Verso, pencil sketch for *The Idle 'Prentice Returned from Sea, and in a garret with a common prostitute* (pl. VIII of the series).

Provenance: The Marquess of Exeter; Edward Speelman 1962.

Literature: A. P. Oppé, *Drawings of William Hogarth*, 1948, no. 57, pl. 50.

Exhibited: V.M.F.A., Richmond, 1963, no. 394.

This subject was not engraved.

The sketch on the verso is the earliest known version of the subject, and another similar preliminary sketch in the British Museum (1914–6-13-30 verso) has details that conform to the more finished drawing there (1896–7-10-16).

James Seymour (1702–1752)

Seymour was born in 1702, the son of James Seymour, a banker and amateur artist whose friends had included Lely, Faithorne, and Sir Christopher Wren. Although Seymour had no formal artistic training, he became one of the most popular sporting artists of his time. He is particularly associated with Newmarket, where he painted portraits of racehorses, many of which were engraved. His painting of the famous carriage match against time at Newmarket in 1750 was once in the collection of Sir Joshua Reynolds (another version is now in the Mellon Collection). Seymour's patrons included Sir William Joliffe, a director of the Bank of England and a keen sportsman, and the Duke of Somerset, who commissioned him to decorate a room at Petworth with portraits of his racehorses. Seymour's work in oils, though inelegant and somewhat coarse in technique, abounds with energy and rhythm. His rapid pen and pencil sketches of horses and other animals moving at speed or in repose, riders, details of dress, and gestures of attendants are bold and expressive, and were useful to Seymour as reportage, for as Shaw Sparrow points out, he understood the value of minor interests and episodes in his racing and sporting scenes. Walpole considered Seymour "too idle to apply himself to his profession"; that he had a relaxed rather than a lazy attitude to life, and particularly to his patrons, is suggested by the shrewd comment inscribed above the exhibited sketches. Seymour died on 30 June 1752.

20 SKETCHES OF A HARE, HORSE, STAG, MAN, AND WOMAN

Pen and sepia ink. 9¾ x 8 inches (24.7 x 20.2 cm.)

Inscribed: *The best Manners is to give the least Trouble / & not to be too Ceremonious* upper right.

Provenance: Sabin Galleries 1961.

Exhibited: V.M.F.A., Richmond, 1963, no. 398, as *Figure and Animal Studies with inscription.*

Samuel Scott (c.1702–1772)

Scott, according to his pupil William Marlow, was born in London. Nothing is known about his upbringing or what led him to painting for a profession. His earliest known painting is dated 1729 and he is generally classified as a marine painter in the manner of Van de Velde, but he also made many pictures of London, especially from viewpoints on the Thames. George Lambert collaborated with Scott in painting in skies and landscapes of his marine and river subjects, notably in a series of East India Settlements. Two well-known painters served as his pupils, William Marlow for five years and Sawrey Gilpin for seven years. He purchased a post in the Stamp Office which yielded £100 a year in return for a few hours' attendance a week, which freed him from relying on painting as a sole source of livelihood. Scott's experience of sea travel was limited to a trip to Helvoetsluys on the yacht that brought George II to England, but this may have kindled his partiality for sea and river scenes.

Scott was one of Hogarth's four companions on the famous "Peregrination" (see Hogarth), for which record he made two watercolors. Lines from William Gostling's transcription of Forrest's account of the frolic give pointers to Scott's character, such as "knowing well his warmth of temper" and (while the others in the party were resting and smoking),

> More diligent and curious, Scott
> Into the forecastle had got
> And took his papers out to draw
> Some ships which right ahead he saw.

By 1746, Canaletto was in London making paintings of the capital veneered with Venetian sunshine, with Anglicized figures bustling, and lightermen in place of gondoliers. The example and demand for these compositions turned Scott to painting large canvases of London views, but in a manner characteristic of himself and not Canaletto. Conversely, as the construction of certain buildings shown in Canaletto's paintings predated his coming to London, it is surmised that he used Scott's drawings as a basis.

Watercolors by Scott are usually unfinished and in restrained coloring. Their rarity makes it difficult to judge Walpole's nomination of Scott as the "father" of English watercolors, a term claimed for several early users of the medium.

Scott exhibited on few occasions; one of his works, an oil, *A View of the Tower of London*, was shown at the Royal Academy the year before he died in Bath on 12 October 1772.

21 A SHIP'S BOAT

Watercolor. 6¼ x 13⅛ inches (15.8 x 33.5 cm.). Watermark *Van der Lay*, c.1724 (Churchill, *Watermarks*, no. 432).

Provenance: L. A. Dorant; L. G. Duke (D.2540), sold Sotheby's, 29 April 1971, lot 150; John Baskett 1971.

Literature: W. R. Jeudwine, "Three Studies by Samuel Scott in the Collection of L. G. Duke Esq., C.B.E.," *Apollo*, November 1956, p. 151, fig. II (fig. III is also now in the Mellon Collection).

Exhibited: Guildhall Art Gallery, *Samuel Scott*, 1956, no. 56.

L. G. Duke notes that this drawing is a study for the boat and crew in the left-center foreground of Scott's painting *A Flagship Shortening Sail* (formerly entitled *The Royal William at Sea*) in the National Maritime Museum, Greenwich. Two more drawings by Scott for this boat are known: one in the Mellon Collection shows two boats approaching a moorage and each carrying twelve men, and the other at the Huntington Library shows a boat with eleven men.

William Taverner (1703–1772)

Taverner was the son of William Taverner, a dramatist and Procurator-General of the Court of Arches of Canterbury. He succeeded his father to this post but devoted his leisure to painting. Little is known of events in his life. He had a bashful reluctance to showing his efforts in painting, and is not to be found in any exhibition records. Vertue said he had a "wonderfull genius to drawing of Landskap in an excellent manner, adorned with figures in a Stile above the common." To a certain extent he was an imitator of Claude and Poussin, and some of his English compositions of the countryside with buildings are translated into classical landscapes with draped figures. Martin Hardie claims him "as our first regular and systematic painter of free landscape in water-colour."

Taverner's work in body color, compared with those in that medium by other artists, is restrained in coloring but achieves rich and satisfying results. His work is rarely dated, does not exist in quantity, and for these reasons it is difficult to trace his development. He died on 20 October 1772.

22 LANDSCAPE WITH BUILDINGS: POSSIBLY AT RICHMOND, SURREY

Watercolor and body color. 9½ x 28 inches (24.2 x 71.2 cm.), on two conjoined sheets of paper.
Provenance: Iolo A. Williams; Colnaghi 1964.
Exhibited: Victoria, 1971, no. 40.

Francis Hayman, R.A. (1708–1776)

Hayman was born in Exeter. He was a pupil of Robert Brown, a portrait painter there, but came early to London and found employment as a scene-painter at Drury Lane. Jonathan Tyers, the proprietor of Vauxhall Gardens, commissioned him to decorate the Rotunda, the loggias, and theatre with scenes of contemporary life. This work did much for Hayman's reputation and led to commissions for historical paintings. The French mode of painting seen in Hayman's pictures was instilled in him by Hubert Gravelot, a fellow teacher at St. Martin's Lane Academy; but Hogarth's influence prevailed in Hayman's portrait groups and theatrical scenes. He was a founder-member of the Society of Artists (and later President) as well as being a founder-member of the Royal Academy, where he became the Librarian. He was among the artists who presented paintings to the Foundling Hospital, a *Finding of Moses* being his contribution.

Hayman made many designs for book illustrations, notably for the works of Shakespeare, Milton, Congreve, Pope, and Smollett. His work was viewed appreciatively and his character with tolerance. To Walpole he was unappealing: rough as a man, and as a painter "a strong mannerist and easily distinguishable by the large noses and shambling legs of his figures." But Edward Dayes considered him as "the venerable father of the English school" as well as "the English Cimabue." He was a man with an enormous appetite, who greatly enjoyed society and the theatre. His later days were plagued by gout. He died in Soho, London, on 2 February 1776 at the age of 68.

23 FIGURES PLAYING SHUTTLECOCK IN AN INTERIOR

Pen and ink and gray wash, squared in pencil. 6⅞ x 9½ inches (17.4 x 24 cm.). Verso, back view of a man, (?) playing a game. Pencil.

Provenance: Henry Reitlinger 1954 (Lugt 2274a); other properties, sold Sotheby's 19 June 1969, lot 160; John Baskett 1969.

Literature: Lawrence Gowing, "Hogarth, Hayman and the Vauxhall Decorations," *Burlington Magazine*, January 1953, p. 11.

Exhibited: Kenwood, *Francis Hayman*, 1963, no. 32.

Engraved: By N. Parr, in the same direction as the drawing.

This is a study for one of Hayman's paintings for the decoration of Vauxhall Gardens.

Allan Ramsay (1713–1784)

Ramsay was born in Edinburgh on 13 October 1713, son of Allan Ramsay, master wigmaker and poet. The literary environment of his home enhanced his education, and his later accomplishments in painting and writing were complemented by his fluency in French, German, Italian, Greek, and Latin. His instruction in painting came from the Academy of St. Luke in Edinburgh under Richard Cooper, the engraver, and possibly from James Norie, the painter. Ramsay's first visit to Italy was in 1736 for two years, in the company of Alexander Cunyngham (later Sir Alexander Dick, Bt.), a young doctor, cultured and bright. Incidents to Ramsay during this period ranged from enduring a shipwreck to meeting Prince Charles Edward, the Young Pretender. Back in London in 1739 he set himself up as a portrait painter in Covent Garden and had the good fortune to be introduced into society by Dr. Richard Mead, connoisseur and the physician to George I. Ramsay soon became the leading portrait painter to the town, a reputation he held for some ten years before the rise of Reynolds. He was a governor of the Foundling Hospital in company with Hogarth, Hudson, Hayman, and other established painters. Again in Italy from 1754 to 1757, he studied the old master paintings to be better equipped against the rivalry of Reynolds. Some of his literary works caused a stir, notably a pamphlet which was instrumental in bringing a popular heroine of abduction, Elizabeth Canning, to trial and conviction for perjury. Her previous evidence had been lurid and false and had almost led to the execution of one of the two maligned women, albeit an undesirable procuress. Another piece of writing criticizing Hogarth's *Analysis of Beauty* led, at least for a time, to an estrangement between the two artists, Hogarth hitting back in caricature with "Mr. Ram's Eye" which appeared in his print, *Battle of Pictures*.

Ramsay became Court Painter on the accession of George III in 1760, and his painting activities were absorbed in meeting the demand for royal portraits from life and in replica. Although he can be counted as one of the great portrait painters in England, he was, according to Alistair Smart, his biographer, "the most unequal of painters, and a consistently high standard must not be looked for in his work." He became ill in Italy in 1784 and, traveling home as quickly as possible to see his daughter who was about to leave for India, he died on landing at Dover on 10 August of that year.

24 HEAD OF A GIRL
Black chalk on blue paper. 12½ x 10½ inches (31.8 x 26.7 cm.)
Provenance: T. E. Lowinsky (Lugt 2420a); Justin Lowinsky; Colnaghi 1963.

Richard Wilson, R.A. (1714–1782)

Wilson was born on 1 August 1714 in Penegoes, Montgomeryshire. His father, the Reverend John Wilson, a man of some social standing, saw to it that his son had a sound classical education. There is no record of Wilson attending a school. He was indentured in 1729 to a little-known portrait painter in London, Thomas Wright, who is sometimes confused with a namesake who wrote a biography of Wilson in 1824. Living in Covent Garden's *Piazza*, then the literary and artistic hub of London, the elegant young Wilson enrolled at St. Martin's Lane Academy and seemed set for a career in fashionable portraiture. It is probable that his friend William Lock impressed in Wilson's mind the thought of changing from portraits to landscapes. In 1750 Wilson arrived in Venice, then enjoying its heyday in art under the great masters Canaletto, Guardi, and Tiepolo. Zuccarelli became a friend and most probably brought Wilson into the company of these three artists. After a year in Venice, he went to Rome with Lock and encountered a realm of light, color, and antiquity that echoed in all that was best in his painting thenceforth. His success followed these responses to the beauty of the fertile landscape, illuminated by the golds and blues from the Italian sky. It was a mental invigoration that has affected so many artists from less exotic lands.

Thoroughly mature and on top of his profession, Wilson ambled back at a leisurely pace to England in 1756, making a lengthy stay with the Earl of Dartmouth at Naples before completing his journey through Germany and Holland. But once back, things went wrong for him in London. The royal approbation, so necessary for the esteem and success of a fashionable painter, was lost by Wilson's attitudes and arrogance. There are many anecdotes written at the time which supply reasons for his decline, from his antagonism to Reynolds to his moving to a seedy dwelling away from the Covent Garden area, and deteriorating into a shambling figure, drinking too much, and unapproachable. Even so, from these accounts there emerges another side of him which shows an amalgam of intelligence above the normal, unswerving beliefs, and refined standards. These qualities were totally unrecognized by an arbitrarily formed "Committee of Taste" which condemned his work as "not suited to English taste."

In 1776, on the death of Francis Hayman, he managed to attain the post of Librarian to the Royal Academy, which was a bare living. On receipt of a small inheritance from his brother he retired to a house near Mold in Flintshire. Here he died on 15 May 1782 after less than a year's residence, leaving a life as dramatic as a *Progress* by Hogarth, wherein a genius in art is overtaken and defeated by a misfit in temperament.

25 TEMPLE OF MINERVA MEDICI, ROME, 1754

Black and white chalk. 11¼ x 16½ inches (28.5 x 41.8 cm.)

Inscribed: On old mount *R. Wilson f. 1754* lower left, *T. of Minerva / Medici* center, and *N⁰ 19* lower right.

Provenance: The Earl of Dartmouth; Agnew 1961.

Literature: Brinsley Ford, *The Drawings of Richard Wilson*, 1951, pl. 55; W. G. Constable, *Richard Wilson*, 1953, no. 88b; Brinsley Ford, "The Dartmouth Collection of Drawings by Richard Wilson," *Burlington Magazine*, vol. 90, p. 345, pl. XIX.

Exhibited: Tate Gallery, *Richard Wilson and his Circle*, 1949, no. 87; National Gallery, Washington, 1962, no. 98.

This drawing is one of a series made in 1754 for the second Earl of Dartmouth, first mentioned in the Earl's correspondence with Thomas Jenkins, his agent in Rome, who may have brought Wilson to Dartmouth's notice. Sixty-eight drawings were commissioned, but only twenty-five have been found. A *Temple of Minerva Medici* by Wilson from the Whitworth Art Gallery was exhibited at the Victoria and Albert Museum, *Englishmen in Italy*, 1968, no. 70.

26 STUDY OF AN ANCIENT TREE

Pencil, heightened with white chalk. 15⅛ x 21⅞ inches (38.5 x 55.5 cm.)

Provenance: The Earl of Warwick (Lugt 2600); Mrs. Arthur Clifton; Agnew 1964.

Alexander Cozens (c.1717–1786)

Alexander Cozens was born in Russia, the son of Richard Cozens, a shipbuilder who was employed by Peter the Great. He was in England in 1742, as shown by a print of Eton College on which his name is inscribed as draughtsman, and probably returned to Russia before traveling to Rome, where he is known to have been living by 1746. In Rome he was a regular visitor to the studio of Claude-Joseph Vernet. In 1746 he returned to London via Germany, where he suffered the misfortune of losing from his saddlebag all the drawings he had made in Rome. In 1749 he was appointed drawing-master at Christ's Hospital, but complaints were made about his teaching and he resigned in 1754. In 1760 he started exhibiting with the Society of Arts and in 1763 transferred to the Society of Artists. From 1772 he exhibited at the Royal Academy, and offered himself twice unsuccessfully for associate membership.

Cozens was established at Eton as an "Extra Master" for drawing by 1766. He was held in wide esteem as an instructor. He devised a number of drawing systems including *A New Method of Assisting the Invention in Drawing Original Compositions of Landscape*, published without date toward the end of his life. His "blottesque" compositions frequently bear the same breadth and simplicity as Chinese drawings. It may have been this element of Oriental romanticism that excited the imagination of the young William Beckford, with whom Cozens formed a friendly association. Cozens died suddenly on 23 April 1786.

27 MOUNTAINOUS LANDSCAPE
Pen and sepia wash. 9½ x 12½ inches (24.1 x 31.7 cm.), on contemporary mount.
Provenance: John Baskett 1970.

Thomas Sandby, R.A. (1723–1798)

Thomas Sandby was born in Nottingham in 1723. Self-taught in both architecture and drawing, he went to London as a young man and obtained a post in the Military Drawing Office in the Tower. As military draughtsman, he accompanied the Commander-in-Chief, William, Duke of Cumberland, on his campaigns in Flanders and Scotland, and was present at several of the Duke's battles (his sketch of the battlefield of Culloden is preserved at Windsor Castle). In 1746 the Duke was appointed Ranger of Windsor Great Park, and shortly afterwards appointed Thomas Sandby Deputy Ranger. Thomas Sandby's work at Windsor, as architect, landscape gardener, and topographical draughtsman, was to be his major preoccupation for fifty years, though he made regular visits to London. He was a foundation member of the Royal Academy and, in 1770, its first Professor of Architecture. His nine exhibits at the Royal Academy were all of buildings. He died at Windsor on 25 June 1798.

Though not as poetic an artist as his brother Paul, Thomas Sandby was a highly competent draughtsman with a sure sense of perspective. His drawings are factual: it is their supreme clarity which gives them elegance. Their attractiveness lies in a technique succinctly analyzed by A. P. Oppé as "sharp contour, precise line, flat wash, fine detail and strong shadow." Thomas and Paul Sandby sometimes collaborated on drawings, and often lent their individual skills (Thomas' in architectural detail, and Paul's in animated foreground figures) to each other's work.

28 WHITEHALL SHOWING HOLBEIN'S GATE AND THE BANQUETING HALL
Watercolor. 15½ x 23½ inches (39.5 x 59.7 cm.)
Provenance: Gardner; Boney; Edward Speelman 1962.
Literature: Dr. Sheppard, *The Old Royal Palace of Whitehall*, 1902, ill. facing p. 8.

22

Exhibited: V.M.F.A., Richmond, 1963, no. 67; Colnaghi, 1964–65, and Yale University Art Gallery, 1965, no. 14; Victoria, 1971, no. 37, pl. 8.

"Whitehall Gate" or "the Cock-pit Gate" was designed by Hans Holbein for one of Henry VIII's additions to Whitehall. It connected the Tennis Court, the Cock-pit, and the Bowling-green with the Palace. It was pulled down in 1759 in order to widen the street.

29 ST. PAUL'S, COVENT GARDEN, SEEN THROUGH THE ARCHES OF THE PIAZZA

Watercolor. 19¾ x 15⅞ inches (50.2 x 40.2 cm.)
Provenance: L. G. Duke (D.1477); Colnaghi 1961.
Exhibited: National Gallery, Washington, 1961, no. 77 (ill.)

Thomas Sandby made several such vistas from under these arches. One was exhibited at the Royal Academy in 1771 (no. 172). Others are at Windsor (Oppé, no. 164) and the British Museum (L.B. 3, 17, 18, 19).

Sir Joshua Reynolds, P.R.A. (1723–1792)

Reynolds was born in Plympton-Earls, Devonshire, on 16 July 1723, son of the Reverend Samuel Reynolds, master of a grammar school. He was apprenticed to Thomas Hudson, portrait painter, in London from 1740 to 1743. From then on he was painting portraits in London and Plymouth. At the invitation of Lord Keppel in 1749 he sailed in the *Centurion*, visiting Spain, Algiers, and Minorca where he fell with his horse down a precipice, sustaining a permanent scar to his upper lip. He went on to Florence and Rome for two years, copying Titian, Rembrandt, Raphael, and other masters. While painting in the Vatican he contracted deafness through the intense cold there, which affected him permanently. Back in London in 1752 he lived in Thornhill's old house in St. Martin's Lane, and in a few years he was outpacing rival portrait painters by his competence. Very soon he was patronized by the royal family and the rich, and his agreeable personality and bright intellect promoted him to the coteries of rank, fashion, and literature. Dr. Samuel Johnson, Oliver Goldsmith, and David Garrick were his lifelong friends, and although he worked for the betterment in standing of his fellow-artists, they were not his consorts in leisure. His success fostered his independence of spirit and, even if the King, George III, found this not to his liking, he nevertheless approved Reynolds' becoming the first President of the Royal Academy on its foundation in 1768. His move in 1760 to a house in Leicester Fields, which he extended with painting-rooms and galleries, was opened with an ostentatious ball, quite uncharacteristic of Reynolds but no doubt demanded by society. He maintained a neutrality in politics, making likenesses of Whig and Tory; and he avoided partiality in the class strata by having bishops and actresses among his sitters. Reynolds reigned, not only over the Academy but throughout the realm in matters of art. His "Discourses" were a revelation in teaching, especially to aspiring artists on the art form that infused a classical and historical mannerism, rapidly becoming acceptable to patrons; and these writings were applauded at home and abroad. There was much parry and thrust between Reynolds and Hogarth, and later from Blake came vitriolic invective on his teachings, the divergence of their ardent ideals in art making this understandable. Reynolds' portraiture stands supreme as the embodiment of the poise and elegance of the eighteenth century.

His eyesight failed him after 1789, and he was then suffering from a disease of the liver; his last two years at the Academy were clouded by disagreement, but his worth there and everywhere was never in doubt. In 1792, the Council minutes record: "On the 23rd of Feb^y 'twixt Eight and Nine in the Evening Died Our Worthy President."

30 STUDY FOR A SELF-PORTRAIT

Black, white, and red chalk on brown paper. 16⅝ x 13½ inches (42.2 x 34.2 cm.)

Inscribed: Verso by Edward Dayes *Sir Joshua Reynolds / given by Ly Inchquin / to E. Dayes.*

Provenance: Lady Inchquin, Reynolds' niece and executrix; Edward Dayes; L. G. Duke (D.2906); Spink 1962.

Exhibited: National Gallery, Washington, 1962, no. 52; V.M.F.A., Richmond, 1963, no. 490; Colnaghi, 1964–65, and Yale University Art Gallery, 1965, no. 69 (ill.).

This is a study for Reynolds' self-portrait in oils, of which there are two versions in the Royal collection. Both were acquired by the Prince Regent; one version is said to have been presented by Reynolds to Burke, and the second was presented to the Prince Regent by Lady Thormond, who described it as the best portrait Reynolds ever painted of himself.

George Stubbs, A.R.A. (1724–1806)

Stubbs was born in Liverpool on 25 August 1724, the son of a currier. At fifteen he was apprenticed to Hamlet Winstanley, but his independent character made this tie of brief duration, and Stubbs progressed with painting through his own diligence and study. Portrait painting was his mainstay until he went to York in his mid-twenties. He then turned to anatomy, a natural switch for a young man who must often have observed the very structure of a horse after flaying, and who early had had encouragement from a doctor to draw human remains. He lectured on anatomy to medical students and, in 1751, illustrated John Burton's book on midwifery with his first efforts at etching. From York he went for two years to Hull, and in 1754 sailed for Rome. Unlike those artists who imbibed the offerings of classical antiquity and the influence of Claude and Poussin while there, Stubbs remained unmoved but came away convinced that nature was to be his future guide.

Back in his native Liverpool in about 1758, he met the companion of his lifetime, Mary Spencer, who was to share in the grisly labor necessary to his anatomical investigation of the horse, and to be the mother of his son, George Townley Stubbs. His plans for his work *The*

Anatomy of the Horse called for rigid determination and desolate living, and the task took over six years. He himself had to engrave the plates, as no engraver would undertake them for fear of ridicule, but the work emerged as a masterpiece of delicate exactness and, when published in 1776, was generally acclaimed. Stubbs had by then been in London for about seven years, painting under the patronage of several sporting noblemen. His portraits of horses, superb in grace and attitude, painted with a full understanding of their physique, set new and high standards for painters in that field.

From 1769 Stubbs became absorbed with experiments in enamel painting and found encouragement for this venture from Josiah Wedgwood who had a similar searching mind and moved in a circle of thinkers and inventors.

In engraving, especially in mezzotint, Stubbs excelled; few engravers could effect such a perfect balance in tones needed to reflect a painting in a print. His ingenuity in using unconventional methods in engraving achieved the results he aimed for. His son, a most proficient engraver, made many plates from his father's paintings.

Stubbs exhibited each year at the Society of Artists from 1761 to 1774, and constantly at the Royal Academy between 1775 and 1802, but although elected an Associate in 1780, a disagreement with the Academy prevented him from becoming a full Academician. He worked on a monumental book, *Comparative Anatomical Exposition of the Human Body with that of a Tiger and a Common Fowl*, from 1795 until he died. Only two numbers were published with ten illustrations altogether, but with no text. The manuscripts and drawings were lost to sight until 1957 when they were located in the Free Public Library in Worcester, Massachusetts.

The end of Stubbs's long life was spent in reduced circumstances but he was, apparently, as stoical in dying as he was purposeful in living. He died in London on 10 July 1806, aged 81.

31 STUDY FOR A SELF-PORTRAIT

Plumbago on squared paper. 12 x 9 inches (30.5 x 23 cm.)

Inscribed: *George Stubbs* on the palette; verso, in a later hand *This is the portrait of George Stubbs / the Animal Painter / and His name is to be seen / on the palette. 5 July 1842 / Capital drawing / by whom?*

Provenance: H. S. Reitlinger (Lugt 2274a on verso); Ian Fleming-Williams 1962.

Literature: Basil Taylor, *Stubbs*, 1971, frontispiece.

Exhibited: V.M.F.A., Richmond, 1963, no. 332; Colnaghi, 1964–65, and Yale University Art Gallery, 1965, no. 6.

This is the drawing for Stubbs's self-portrait in enamel on a ceramic tablet, in the National Portrait Gallery, London. The enamel is dated 1781, and measures 27 x 20 inches.

32 HORSES FIGHTING

Gray wash. 17⅛ x 23¼ inches (43.5 x 59.1 cm.)

Provenance: Basil Taylor; Colnaghi 1964.

Engraved: In mezzotint by George Townley Stubbs, published 1 May 1788, a companion print to *Bulls Fighting*.

25

33 A PRANCING HORSE

Red chalk. 8¾ x 9½ inches (22 x 24 cm.)

Provenance: Sold Sotheby's, 3 May 1961, lot 7; Colnaghi 1961.

Exhibited: National Gallery, Washington, 1962, no. 82; V.M.F.A., Richmond, 1963, no. 333; Colnaghi, 1964–65, and Yale University Art Gallery, 1965, no. 52.

Thomas Gainsborough, R.A. (1727–1788)

Gainsborough was born in the market town of Sudbury, Suffolk, the youngest of the nine children of John Gainsborough, a manufacturer of woollen fabrics. He came to London where he was a pupil of Gravelot. He later set up on his own, and in 1746 married Margaret Burr, an attractive girl who had had a small annuity settled upon her. He returned to his native provincial town in 1748. Four years later he moved with his wife and two young daughters to Ipswich, where he hoped to find better patronage. There he based his practice mostly on portraits of the local gentry and professional classes. He was obliged to send his treasured landscapes to the London art dealer Panton Betew, who put them in his shop window where they sold for shillings. By 1759 Gainsborough's friend Philip Thicknesse had persuaded him to move to Bath, where his business blossomed, and he was moved to write to his close friend William Jackson, the Exeter organist and composer: "I might add perhaps in my red hot way that damn me Exeter is no more a place for a Jackson, than Sudbury in Suffolk is for a G———."

He started exhibiting at the Society of Artists and from 1769 at the Royal Academy, and began to make frequent trips to London. His passion for music and the theatre led him into contact with Karl Friedrich Abel, Johann Christian Bach, and David Garrick. Gainsborough moved to London in 1774. The previous year he had quarreled with the Royal Academy, of which he was a founder-member, and withheld his pictures from their exhibitions until 1777, when he received the first of a series of commissions from the Royal Family and his position both financially and as a painter was assured. With this security he branched out in the last decade of his life with experiments in print-making, "fancy" pictures, and transparencies. He died of cancer after a short illness in 1788, aged 61.

34 WOODED LANDSCAPE WITH GYPSY ENCAMPMENT

Watercolor and body color over pencil on pale brown prepared paper. 11¼ x 9¼ inches (28.7 x 23.5 cm.)

Provenance: Mrs. Donald (née Osborne); Miss Treacher; Colnaghi 1962.

Literature: John Hayes, *The Drawings of Thomas Gainsborough*, 1971, no. 276, pl. 88.

Exhibited: National Gallery, Washington, 1962, no. 36; V.M.F.A., Richmond, 1963, no. 61; Colnaghi, 1964–65, and Yale University Art Gallery, 1965, no. 13, ill.

Dr. Hayes notes in his catalogue raisonné that the treatment of the foliage and the lighting are related to Gainsborough's painting of the mid-1760's.

35 OPEN LANDSCAPE WITH HORSEMEN AND COVERED CART

Gray and gray-black washes, with traces of black and white chalk. 10¾ x 14 inches (27.5 x 35.5 cm.)

Inscribed: Verso *No. 3* in pencil, top left.

Provenance: Bruce Ingram (Ingram sale, Foster's, 18 June 1930, lot 19a, part of a parcel); L. G. Duke (D.606); Colnaghi 1960.

Literature: Mary Woodall, *Gainsborough's Landscape Drawings*, 1963, no. 41; John Hayes, *The Drawings of Thomas Gainsborough*, 1971, no. 507, pl. 161.

Exhibited: Sassoon, *Gainsborough*, 1936, no. 61; Aldeburgh, 1949, no. 6; South London Art Gallery, *English Landscape Drawing and Painting*, 1951, no. 45; Arts Council, *Three Centuries of British Water-colours and Drawings*, 1951, no. 75; Orangerie, Paris, *Le Paysage Anglais de Gainsborough à Turner*, 1953, no. 52; National Gallery, Washington, 1962, no. 35; V.M.F.A., Richmond, 1963, no. 60.

36 WOODED LANDSCAPE WITH FIGURES

Black chalk and stump with some red chalk, and gray and brown washes, on buff paper, touched with body color. 15½ x 12½ inches (39.4 x 31.7 cm.)

Provenance: T. E. Lowinsky (Lugt 2420a); Justin Lowinsky; Colnaghi 1963.

Literature: Mary Woodall, *Gainsborough's Landscape Drawings*, 1939, no. 208; John Hayes, *The Drawings of Thomas Gainsborough*, 1971, no. 803, pl. 349.

Exhibited: Louvre, Paris, *La Peinture Anglaise*, 1938, no. 199; Arts Council, *Three Centuries of British Water-colours and Drawings*, 1951, no. 74; Royal Academy, *Drawings by Old Masters*, 1953, no. 444; Arts Council, *Gainsborough Drawings*, 1960–61, no. 57, pl. vi.

This drawing is a study for the painting *The Cottage Door, with a Peasant Smoking* in the University of California at Los Angeles (see Ellis Waterhouse, *Gainsborough*, 1958, no. 1011, pl. 285). The essentials for the composition are contained in the drawing, but the painting varies in detail. The painting is dated 1788; Waterhouse points out that it was the last landscape of any importance painted by Gainsborough and was designed as a companion to *The Market Cart*, exhibited for sale at Schomberg House in 1789.

37 STUDY OF ROCKS AND PLANTS

Black chalk, with watercolor and gouache. 9 x 11⅛ inches (23 x 28.2 cm.). Watermark *fleur-de-lys*, n.d.

Provenance: David Rolt (a descendant of Dr. Monro); Colnaghi 1962.

Literature: John Hayes, *The Drawings of Thomas Gainsborough*, 1971, no. 311, pl. 107, p. 180.

Exhibited: V.M.F.A., Richmond, 1963, no. 58 (ill.); Colnaghi, 1964–65, and Yale University Art Gallery, 1965, no. 12.

Dr. Hayes dates this drawing to the late 1760's, Gainsborough's Bath period, and relates the cursory handling of the foreground to that in the drawing of *A Wooded Landscape with a Boy reclining in a Cart* in the British Museum (1896–5-11-2).

Paul Sandby, R.A. (1730–1809)

Paul Sandby was born in Nottingham on 12 January 1730, younger brother of Thomas (q.v.). When Paul was seventeen, Thomas, who had preceded him to London, secured for him a post in the Military Drawing Office of the Tower of London. He was later appointed draughtsman to a survey for roads in the Highlands of Scotland. While in Scotland he developed a skill in etching, an art he extended by experiment from a "secret" passed to him by the Hon. Charles Greville, the result being named by him *aquatinta*. The first innovator of this process in England, he produced prints that stimulated engravers to exploit the medium, the graduated tones of which proved suitable for imitating watercolors. He etched caricatures in a battle with Hogarth over the latter's *Analysis of Beauty*, but as Sandby respected and admired Hogarth's invention and skill in painting, he lacked the venom for them to be effectual.

Sandby lived for long periods with his brother at Windsor, and some of his finest watercolors were of the Castle and the vicinity surrounding the Park. He was in great favor with George III, and members of the royal family were among his many distinguished pupils. James Gandon, his architect friend, says that Sandby's house attracted assemblies of friends forming *conversazioni* on the arts, sciences and literature of the day. With prodigious industry he journeyed all over Britain drawing buildings of interest and beauty from which he made compositions that encompassed the classical form of the time and topographical fact. In the foreground of his pictures were graceful knolls and sturdy oaks, sculpted by storms. His experiments with pigments even included scraping some burnt breakfast toast and mixing it with gum to make an effective tone of black. More than any artist, he developed watercolor as a major satisfying pictorial expression, from the usual pen drawing "stained" with watercolor. Hitherto, oil-painting had been the medium acceptable for exhibition, and Sandby's works shown at the Society of Arts and the Royal Academy from 1760 to 1809 provided the impetus needed to popularize the art of watercolor.

Sandby retired as drawing-master from the Royal Military College at Woolwich to live at Paddington until his death on 7 November 1809.

38 THE NORMAN GATE, WINDSOR CASTLE

Watercolor. 15 x 21⅛ inches (38 x 53.5 cm.)

Provenance: H.R.H. The Princess Royal, presented to her, on the occasion of her marriage, by the Hon. Sir Richard Molyneux K.C.V.O.; 7th Earl of Harewood, sold Christie's 13 July 1965, lot 170 (ill.); Colnaghi 1965.

Literature: T. Borenius, *The Harewood Collection*, 1936, no. 427.

A variant of this drawing in pencil and watercolor with some body-color, and from a closer viewpoint, is at Windsor (Oppé, no. 13, pl. 6).

39 ROSSLYN CASTLE, NORTH BERWICK

Watercolor and body color. 17¾ x 24⅝ inches (45 x 62.5 cm.)

Provenance: Herbert Peake; William Sandby; Agnew 1960.

Exhibited: V.M.F.A., Richmond, 1963, no. 69.

There is a small study, also in the Mellon collection, of the woman drawing with the aid of a camera lucida.

40 AN ENCAMPMENT IN ST. JAMES'S PARK

Watercolor. 11⅞ x 17⅞ inches (30.2 x 45.5 cm.), on an early mount.

Provenance: 6th Earl of Harewood; 7th Earl of Harewood, sold Christie's 13 July 1965, lot 168 (ill.); Colnaghi 1965.

Literature: T. Borenius, *The Harewood Collection*, 1936, no. 432.

Exhibited: Royal Academy, 1781, no. 371; Victoria, 1971, no. 36.

The Guards were assembled in London parks on account of the Gordon Riots in 1780. This drawing is one of a set of four of similar encampments in Hyde Park, Museum Gardens, and Blackheath; the latter is in the British Museum (L.B. 111). All four were reproduced in aquatint and printed in color by Sandby himself. This encampment is of the 5th Battalion of Guards: in the tent on the right is Colonel Woodford; in the other tent is Lt. Col. Greville, both of the 1st Regiment of Foot Guards.

41 NORTH-WEST VIEW OF WAKEFIELD LODGE IN WHITTLEBURY FOREST, 1767

Watercolor. 16⅝ x 33⅜ inches (42.3 x 84.9 cm.)

Inscribed: *P. Sandby 1767* in gold, lower right.

Provenance: Lady Hillingdon; Agnew 1967.

Two views of Wakefield Lodge by Sandby were exhibited at the Society of Artists in 1767, cat. no. 272.

George Romney (1734–1802)

Romney was born on 26 December 1734 at Dalton-le-Furness, Lancashire, the son of a carpenter, builder, and farmer. He was apprenticed to a cabinetmaker, developed a skill in wood carving, and even made himself a fiddle. He was early undecided whether to make music or painting his profession. He was pupil to a portrait painter, Christopher Steele, an unstable character who assumed the title of "Count." At twenty-two Romney married, and for five years painted portraits and landscapes, living meanwhile in Kendal. But his income was small and he believed his marital commitments were jeopardizing his progress and ambitions; therefore in 1762, he left his family and made for London. To raise money for this venture, he sold twenty of his paintings by lottery.

Established as a portrait painter in London, he saved money for a visit to France where he went in 1764 with his lawyer friend, Thomas Greene. In Paris, Romney studied the masterpieces in the Louvre and met artists, notably Joseph Vernet who acted as his host and guide. It was a stimulating experience which resulted in a livening of his work on his return to London. But it was essential for any aspiring artist to have a background of study in Italy, and this Romney achieved after much hard work and saving. He left for a tour there in 1773 in the company of Ozias Humphry, the miniaturist. They mixed with the artistic fraternity in

Rome: Wright of Derby, Fuseli, and Banks, among the artists and sculptors; Charles Townley, Edward Wortley Montagu, and Richard Payne Knight, among other worthies. The stay in Italy lasted over two years, during which time Romney practiced a neoclassical style of drawing, concentrating on purity of line.

Back in London in July 1775, he took a house in Cavendish Square in which he spent the rest of his working life. He exhibited little and was persuaded by his poet friend William Hayley not to become enmeshed in the distractions associated with the Royal Academy. In 1782, Emma Hart (later Lady Hamilton) was brought to Romney's studio by Charles Greville, to sit for the first of her many portraits made there. Full rein has been given by romantics ever since to her beauty, her notoriety, and her attraction for Romney. By nature inclined to melancholy and hypochondria, Romney lived through this period of volcanic emotional uncertainty in profound distress. This was, fortunately, alleviated by the prospect of painting "history" compositions for Boydell's *Shakespeare Gallery*, work which called for much concentration from him. His character must have appealed generally, but especially to his biographers, Hayley, John Romney his son, Cumberland, and Chamberlain. They all protest strongly if they detect a hint in each other's devoted accounts that Romney could wittingly err; they offer a variety of plausible motives even for Romney's desertion of his wife and family for thirty-seven years. In his failing years Romney returned to his wife at Kendal, who cared for him until he died on 15 November 1802.

Among the thousands of drawings by him that exist are many inventive details for compositions that never reached canvas. His pen drawings with sepia shadows are especially vivid in dramatic groups of figures, while some of his demoniac heads equal the ferocity of Fuseli's; few drawings are identified for known portraits done in oils. His soft-colored portraits, painted to please, their liquid eyes compelling attention away from the rest of the picture, have virtually no relationship with these spontaneous and spirited sketches.

42 "A MOTHER WITH HER CHILD IN HER ARMS, FLYING UPON THE RAMPARTS OF A CITY IN FLAMES"

Sepia wash. 19⅝ x 16 inches (50.8 x 40.7 cm.)

Provenance: Miss Romney, in her sale 1814; T. E. Lowinsky (Lugt 2420a); Justin Lowinsky.

Exhibited: Royal Academy, *British Art*, 1934, no. 618, pl. CLIV.

The title was given by the painter's son, John Romney, to another version of this composition (Fitzwilliam Museum, Cambridge, B.V.28) which he presented, among a representative group of his father's drawings, to the University of Cambridge in 1818. The Fitzwilliam sheet, drawn in pen with brown ink and brown ink wash over pencil, omits the horseman at the right. It is a study for the right-hand group in a painting of unidentified subject, once in the collection of G. Clark, London. In the finished composition Romney showed old men, women, and children fleeing from the firing and destruction of a city by night. The destruction of Troy being the most famous classical incident of this sort, it is tempting to suppose that this is what is here represented; but in the absence of firm evidence it is better to adhere to John Romney's title. John Romney also presented to the University of Cambridge another study for the same painting (Fitzwilliam Museum, Cambridge, B.V.29). Stylistically the drawings and painting belong to the period 1776–77, immediately after Romney's return from Rome.

Jonathan Skelton (c.1735–1759)

Nothing is known about the date and place of Skelton's birth, nor about his early training. Skelton's only reference to a "master" occurs in reported statements, made when he was in Italy, of his intention to paint in his own way and not in his master's manner. Iolo Williams notes a similarity of his early work to that of George Lambert as a possible clue to that master. Drawings made after Skelton left England show the strong influence of Claude Lorrain. He is known to have painted in oils, but though such work should warrant survival under his own name, it must now be resting under names better known. Skelton was in Italy from 1757 and is thought to have attended life classes at the Academy of St. Luke, possibly because he had little success in selling his landscapes, and wrote that only portraits seemed required. He also complained of a conspiracy by a group of rival English painters to ruin him by spreading the rumor that he was a Jacobite; this was entirely false, but it was a ruse frequently used in Italy at that time.

Skelton was unknown in the English School until 1909, when eighty-four of his drawings appeared for sale from the effects of T. C. Blofeld of Hoveton House, near Norwich. A checklist of Skelton's drawings published by the Walpole Society, Volume XXXIV, gives the number known to have existed as eighty-seven, but less than half of these have been located; thus again there are riches by this artist to be uncovered.

Skelton was the first English artist to make watercolors of Rome of anything like such high quality; and the sensitive structure and rich tones of his buildings, whether farmhouse or castle, show him to be the most outstanding artist in watercolor to precede Sandby. Skelton's letters from Rome to his patron, William Herring of Croydon (transcribed in the Walpole Society volume mentioned), give lively and detailed accounts of all that was happening to him. The last letter is dated 23 December 1758; a letter to Herring dated 24 January 1759 from George James, A.R.A., portrait painter and Skelton's friend in Rome, gives a graphic account of Skelton's distressing and painful death from a duodenal ulcer. A pathetic will, made some two months before he died, listed debts to his friends and asked that his effects be divided proportionately among his creditors.

43 HARBLEDOWN, A VILLAGE NEAR CANTERBURY, 1757

Watercolor. 8 x 21¼ inches (20.2 x 53.9 cm.)

Inscribed: On old backing-board *Harbledown, A Village near Canterbury / J: Skelton 1757 / N:B: Drawn immediately after a heavy Summer-Shower.*

Provenance: George Thorne-Drury, K.C.; Mrs. S. M. Cowles; sold Sotheby's 5 July 1966, lot 10; Colnaghi 1966.

Exhibited: Victoria, 1971, no. 38.

Francis Towne (1739 or 1740–1816)

Towne's origins are obscure, but he is believed to have been born in Devonshire. He began to paint in oils at the age of 14, and appears to have been a pupil at Shipley's School in London, with his lifelong friends Cosway and Humphry (both Devonshire men) and William Pars. All the work he exhibited (beginning in 1762 at the Society of Artists, then at the Free Society and later at the Royal Academy) was in oils. He rarely worked in watercolor until 1777, when he made a tour in Wales, and began to evolve a highly distinctive style in that medium. This was to find its highest point of expression in 1780–81, when he traveled to Italy where his friend William Pars had settled, making the return journey in company with John "Warwick" Smith. After his return, Towne divided his time between London and Exeter, where he gave lessons (his best-known pupil was John White Abbott) and executed commissions in oils and watercolors, his patrons throughout being Devonshire men. Towne died in London on 7 July 1816, and was buried in Heavitree churchyard, Exeter.

Towne's reputation rests largely on the drawings he made during his single tour abroad in 1780–81. His manner is strikingly original. Drawings made during his earlier Welsh tour already show his determination to comprehend and define the form and structure of mountain scenery, but are comparatively timidly handled. Switzerland and Italy evoked a far more powerful response. Landscape with a hint of peril or menace in the air—the "crushing grandeur" of the Alps and their slow-moving glaciers, the massive ruins of Rome, anything jagged, shadowed, cleft or riven—excited him to a high pitch of controlled awe. His drawings are remarkable for their austerity of design and sharpness of focus. He does not strive for liveliness, still less for the picturesque; instead he succeeds, with no loss of drama, in eliminating inessentials and (to quote Martin Hardie) "extracting symmetry and order from wild profusion." Most of Towne's watercolors have a basis of sharp, delicate penwork, with a flat patterning of color which, under the Italian light, became bolder and more intense. After his return from Italy Towne produced many good drawings (especially during a tour of the Lakes in 1786) but never again reached the heights of his tour of 1780–81.

44 ENTRANCE TO THE GROTTO AT POSILIPPO, NAPLES, 1781

Watercolor (peasants and sheep outlined in pencil). 12⅝ x 9⅛ inches (32 x 23.2 cm.)

Inscribed: Verso *No. 9. Naples / March 24. 1781 / Francis Towne.*
Provenance: W. H. H. Merivale; Agnew 1967.
Literature: Martin Hardie, I, pl. 102.
Exhibited: Victoria, 1971, no. 41.

A watercolor of this subject, with the same date, is in the British Museum (L.B. IV, p. 203, no. 12).

William Marlow (1740–1813)

Marlow was born in Southwark, London, in 1740. He was Samuel Scott's pupil for five years, then studied at the St. Martin's Lane Academy founded by Hogarth. From Scott's teaching and his own study of Canaletto, Marlow developed the art of London topography, painting many London scenes both in oils and in watercolors. He is particularly associated with views of the Thames and its bridges, not only in the cities of London and Westminster, but also in its higher reaches around Richmond and Twickenham. From 1765 to 1768 he traveled in France and Italy. His paintings and drawings of continental views reveal an admirably flexible approach to new subject-matter. At home his work suggested the gentle, hazy atmosphere of the English climate; abroad, it reflected the stronger, sharper light which bleaches the stone and deepens the shadows of ancient buildings. Paris, Avignon, Nîmes, Florence and the Arno, Rome and the Tiber, Naples, and Venice are notably associated with his work abroad.

Marlow was a member of the Society of Artists (and its Vice-President in 1778), and exhibited some one hundred and twenty-five paintings and drawings there between 1762 and 1790; he also exhibited between 1788 and 1807 at the Royal Academy, but did not seek its membership. In addition to his views, he left many vigorous sketches and figure studies. Binyon remarks that "something of the Hogarthian tradition can be traced in his rather loose drawing; he is always the painter rather than the draughtsman." Marlow's work was popular and brought him financial independence. He emerges as an amiable character. For the last thirty years of his life he lodged at Twickenham with a family named Curtis; Farington observed waspishly in 1808 that there were now in the Twickenham establishment "6 or 7 children, some of them very like Marlow." John Curtis, who exhibited at the Royal Academy between 1790 and 1822, was Marlow's only known pupil. Toward the end of his life Marlow gave up painting, Farington relates, "for an amusement more agreeable to him, the making of telescopes and other articles." He is also said to have designed the seals for the original thirteen United States of America. He died at Twickenham on 14 January 1813.

45 THE AMPHITHEATRE AT NÎMES

Watercolor. 13¼ x 20¼ inches (33.6 x 51.4 cm.)

Inscribed: W. M. lower left.

Provenance: Dr. T. C. Girtin, c.1850; Mrs. Barnard; Mrs. Sutton; T. R. C. Blofield; Tom Girtin; John Baskett 1970.

Exhibited: Arts Council, *Three Centuries of British Water-colours*, 1951, no. 112; Guildhall Art Gallery, *William Marlow*, 1956, no. 72; Leeds City Art Gallery, *Early English Water-colours*, 1958, no. 71.

Another version of this, of almost equal size, is in the collection of Mr. John Mitchell, London, and was shown in his exhibition in aid of Friends of the Courtauld Institute, November 1970–January 1971, no. 28.

John Hamilton Mortimer, A.R.A. (1740–1779)

Mortimer was born at Eastbourne, Sussex, in September 1740, the son of a mill-owner. In 1757 he became the pupil of Thomas Hudson, portrait painter, making a lifelong friend of his fellow-pupil, Joseph Wright of Derby. Later he was a prize-winning student at the St. Martin's Lane Academy and the Duke of Richmond's Gallery; at the age of 23 he won the Society of Arts' first prize for historical painting with his *St. Paul Preaching to the Britons*. Teachers and fellow-students alike regarded him as a prodigy, a draughtsman who could toss off brilliant unconventional figure studies "in the most difficult attitudes that could be devised, & begin at the *heel* . . . but what was still more amazing, he never altered a line: the first stroke always remained untouched . . . and all the time he was thus pouring out wonders, he conversed, & entertained his friends with the same easy cheerfulness & pleasantry as if wholly unemployed." Mortimer first exhibited at the age of 22 at the Society of Artists, and continued exhibiting there (playing a leading part in its politics, and becoming its President in 1774) until 1778, when he was elected to Associate Membership of the Royal Academy; he was up for election as a full member when he died.

Mortimer's early work—portraits, conversation pieces, and historical paintings—was largely in oils, and in a conventional manner. About 1770 he became preoccupied with images of contests between victors and the vanquished, sometimes drawing his themes from ancient history, sometimes devising semi-heroic, semi-brutal episodes for banditti derived from Salvator Rosa, sometimes drawing from his own imagination subhuman monsters which carried human passions to extremes. He drew frontispieces for Bell's *Poets of Great Britain* (1777–79), and scenes from Chaucer and *Don Quixote*. Characteristically his illustrations to Shakespeare were not, in the style of contributors to Boydell's Gallery, representations of incidents but portraits of the protagonists, his Lear and Caliban being particularly dramatic. He himself etched his Shakespeare characters, and much else. He drew self-portraits frequently, depicting himself "in character," in a role half poet, half chief of banditti, challenging the spectator with a romantic image of restless energy. Mortimer lived a full and often reckless life. He enjoyed diversions such as fishing with Benjamin West, playing cricket, or boating excursions with his friend Thomas Jones and others, and had numerous acquaintances among playwrights, sportsmen, actors, artists, and politicians. But there was a darker side to his life, a dissipation (rarely specified) which seriously undermined his health. Marriage in 1775 gave him a few years of more tranquil life before his death in London on 4 February 1779, aged 38.

46 BACK VIEW OF THE ARTIST IN COSTUME, COMPOSING A LETTER

Pen and sepia ink. 21¼ x 16¼ inches (51.5 x 41.3 cm.)

Inscribed: *Rara avis in terra* lower left; *For who can paint this Character as it ought / Tho' Wisdom cryeth out in the Streets yet* [third line illegible] lower center; *Pen & Ink Drawing by Mortimer* in different hand, lower right. The artist portrays himself reading a letter dated *July 26: Hon^d Sir – I flatter myself I have abilities for the Art of Painting w^ch / I hope will appear by the Drawing I send you, but indeed / there are so many young Persons pursuing the same / Art, that I think it will be a prudent step to / drop it intirely, & get into any line of Business / you shall think proper, I make / no doubt but you will comply / with my desire more especially / when you inform yourself how / much the Profession is disgrac'd / by the Folly & Vice of many of / the Professors.* In front of him is a sketch inscribed *Pride led by the / Passions Design for Spensers Faery Queen*; the upper corner is turned over, and inscribed *To Mr. Brind. . . .*

Provenance: George Hilder Libbis; Nell Hilder Libbis, sold Sotheby's 13 March 1969, lot 67; John Baskett 1969.

The use of pen and India ink without wash is a characteristic of Mortimer's drawings. He achieved effects of shadows by stippling dots with the pen, a technique very close to that he used in etching.

George Dance II, R.A. (1741–1825)

Dance was born in London. His father, George Dance senior, was a noted architect who gave early instruction in architecture to his son. From the age of 17, Dance spent seven years studying in Rome, Florence, Naples, and Parma. In 1768 his father died, and Dance succeeded him in the office of Clerk of the City Works in London, by right of purchase. Dance's most famous work was the rebuilding of Newgate Prison. In this he reflected the somberness of the prisons in the dramatic etchings of Piranesi. Dance had met the famous engraver, then at the height of his career, in Rome.

Art rather than architecture was always Dance's inclination, and this grew stronger with age. He was a founder-member of the Royal Academy, and held the post of Professor of Architecture from 1789 to 1805, though he gave no lectures. He was gifted in drawing, and made numerous portraits in pencil, tinged with watercolor, which were sensitive and truthful likenesses. The majority of these were in profile; over seventy of his drawings of eminent persons were engraved and published by William Daniell. Dance also had a talent for caricature, and depicted topical events and amusing situations within high society; but many of the allusions are now lost. His satires were never cruel, biting, or vulgar; they were, rather, of impish or rib-poking fun, and often attractively colored in pinks, greens, and blues. Dance played the violin, the violoncello, and the flute with equal skill, and composed a rousing marching song, *One and All*, which so pleased the Prince of Wales that he ordered it to be played by the band of his regiment. Dance died in London on 14 January 1825, and was buried in St. Paul's Cathedral.

47 PORTRAIT OF A BOY, 1793

Pencil and watercolor. 9⅝ x 7½ inches (24.5 x 19 cm.)

Inscribed: *Geo. Dance* lower right, and dated *Aug.st 3d, 1793* lower left.

Provenance: Colnaghi 1961.

Literature: Martin Hardie, I, pl. 122.

Exhibited: National Gallery, Washington, 1962, no. 28 (ill.); V.M.F.A., Richmond, 1963, no. 406; Colnaghi, 1964–65, and Yale University Art Gallery, 1965, no. 8.

Henry Fuseli, R.A. (1741–1825)

Fuseli was born in February 1741 in Zürich, the second son of Johann Caspar Füssli, painter and writer. The family were lovers of art, poetry, and literature, and had many cultured friends. Fuseli read widely in classical legends and myths, and the fantasy of heroic deeds was rooted deeply in his mind. He absorbed the works of Shakespeare, Milton, Dante, and Rousseau, and was unusually gifted in foreign languages. On encouragement from his parents he took holy orders at the age of 20; two years later, however, he left Switzerland with his friend Johann Kaspar Lavater, the physiognomist, and studied with the philosopher Sulzer in Berlin. He came to England in 1764 with Sir Andrew Mitchell, the British minister, who sponsored him among the eminent writers and artists in London. Reynolds was impressed with his draughtsmanship and urged him to devote his life to painting, and to study art in Italy. Fuseli, following this advice, spent eight years in Italy, returning to England in full mastery of painting and with his fertile imagination stimulated. He was thus well equipped to give full rein to his powers of composition, and "history painting" was the obvious conduit for his ideas. Scope for these came from his commissions for subjects in Boydell's *Shakespeare Gallery* and later for his own creations of a "Milton Gallery" for which he painted forty life-size compositions from the poet's works; but this venture proved a financial failure for him.

With his reputation established, Fuseli was elected an Associate in 1788, and a full member of the Royal Academy in 1790; he later became Professor of Painting and finally Keeper in 1804. He based much of the substance of his Academy lectures on a visit to Paris in 1802 where he studied the rich art treasures plundered by Napoleon. Fuseli was eccentric in character, with a brilliant but caustic wit which made him welcome at dinners and gatherings. His pupils flourished under his teaching, which placed emphasis on evoking their own wish to learn rather than on practical instruction. His favorite axiom was that "time and not the teacher made an artist." He was attractive to women but did not abuse this characteristic, and his female friendships remained long and sincere. Of his work, it is his impetuous drawings, with their exaggerations and vivid shadows, that have recurring impact, rather than his completed compositions on canvas.

Fuseli's health was excellent throughout his long, active, and abstemious life, which ended with his death in London on 16 April 1825.

48 ARIADNE WATCHING THE STRUGGLE OF THESEUS WITH THE MINOTAUR

Brown wash and white body color. 24 x 19¾ inches (61 x 50 cm.)

Provenance: T. E. Lowinsky; Justin Lowinsky 1963.

Literature: J. Piper, *British Romantic Artists*, 1942, ill. p. 27; P. Ganz, *Zeichnungen* . . . *Fusslis*, Berne, 1947, p. 87, and *The Drawings of Henry Fuseli*, 1949, pl. 87; Martin Hardie, i, pl. 207.

Exhibited: Roland, Browse & Delbanco, *Fuseli*, 1948, no. 22; Arts Council, *The Romantic Movement*, 1959, no. 163.

This is probably a study for a painting exhibited at the Royal Academy in 1820 (no. 228). The painting is now in a Swiss private collection.

49 STANDING WOMAN
Watercolor. 14⅜ x 8⅞ inches (36.5 x 22.5 cm.). Watermark *A. Blackwell 1798*.
Inscribed: *Wednesday Septr 181*(?).
Provenance: T. E. Lowinsky (Lugt 2420a); Justin Lowinsky 1963.
Exhibited: V.M.F.A., Richmond, 1963, no. 487.

William Pars, A.R.A. (1742–1782)

Pars was born in London, the son of a metal chaser. At nearly fourteen, in 1756, he was awarded a premium at William Shipley's drawing school where he continued to study until 1761. In that year his brother Henry took over the school, and William acted as an assistant, enrolling at the same time at St. Martin's Lane Academy. As was usual, Pars turned to portraiture for a steady living. He must have had more general accomplishments as a draughtsman, for in 1764 he was chosen to accompany Richard Chandler and Nicholas Revett to Asia Minor, on an expedition commissioned by the Society of Dilettanti, which lasted until August 1776. Some drawings he made of the classical remains in Athens were used for the *Antiquities of Athens*, a work that dealt with the previous expedition of 1752. Figures feature interestingly and naturally in Pars's drawings at this time, probably owing to the examples he must have seen by James "Athenian" Stuart who drew for the 1752 expedition; in his preface Stuart emphasizes "preferring truth to every other consideration," and this applies to the costume of the inhabitants as well as to the remains.

Pars was elected Associate of the Royal Academy in 1770 and in the same year had the satisfaction of being engaged by Lord Palmerston on a grand tour through Switzerland to Italy. His drawings of Swiss scenery preceded those by Francis Towne and John Robert Cozens by a decade, and the different impact that country had on the three artists is remarkable. Towne, returning from Italy with his folio of Roman drawings each full of exultant light and rich shadow, produced awesome effects from the gigantic Alps; Cozens, displaying the same mountains encircling valleys, softens his scene with wooded slopes and misty distances. Pars, more factual by training, achieved rather detached results, and was obviously fascinated by ice formations from the spill of glaciers.

On his return to England, Pars made further tours with Lord Palmerston, taking in Ireland and the Lake District; and he turned again to his original living of portrait painting. From 1775 he was once more in Italy as a student supported by the Dilettanti Society. For a time, Thomas Jones, painter and diarist, shared a house with Pars, and throws some light on his character. Both men were attracted by a "Roman Virgin" who spent most of her time on a balcony of the adjacent house; each artist wrote separate letters to her, and Pars "would cling to the grating of her window for hours together, broiling in the Sun like a Lizard." Throughout the two remained friends despite Pars's being "rather hasty and sometimes indeed violent in his Temper." Jones records that Pars died in October 1782 as the result of standing in the cold water at Tivoli sketching the Grotto of Neptune, and contracting dropsy.

50 ROME FROM THE PINCIAN, 1776

Watercolor. 15⅛ x 21⅛ inches (38.5 x 53.8 cm.)
Inscribed: *W. Pars Rome, 1776* lower left.
Provenance: T. Girtin; Tom Girtin; John Baskett 1970.
Exhibited: Norwich Castle Museum, *A Loan Exhibition of Eighteenth Century Italy and the Grand Tour*, 1958, no. 42; Leeds City Art Gallery, *Early English Water-colours*, 1958, no. 75; Rome, *Settecento*, 1959; Royal Academy, *The Girtin Collection*, 1962, no. 2; Victoria and Albert Museum, *The Englishman in Italy*, 1968, no. 39.

Pars's drawings made for the Asia Minor expedition are disciplined in form and color by comparison with those done in Rome. The companionship of Pars, John "Warwick" Smith, and Francis Towne, often drawing the same scene, helped Pars to develop a freer, lighter touch in his handling of watercolor.

Michael "Angelo" Rooker, A.R.A. (1743–1801)

Rooker was born in London, the son of an engraver, Edward Rooker, whose profession he followed. He studied at St. Martin's Lane Academy, and his friend Paul Sandby, who dubbed him "Angelo," gave him lessons in painting. In 1769 he enrolled as a student at the Royal Academy schools and exhibited two "stained" drawings there in the same year. Although elected as an Associate in the following year, and constantly exhibiting thereafter up to his death, he never achieved the rank of Academician.

Rooker proved an excellent engraver, and for some years contributed attractive topographical views to head the *Oxford Almanack*. His father supplemented his own meager income from engraving by acting in the theatre as "Ned" Rooker, a popular harlequin. It must have been through his father's connection with the theatre that Rooker, on withdrawing from engraving on account of faltering eyesight, became principal scene-painter for George Colman at his theatre in the Haymarket. He was billed to the public in some burlesque productions as "Signor Rookerini."

In 1788 Rooker made the first of a series of walking tours, drawing topography and antiquities in English counties, many of them later engraved. His watercolors are works of precision tempered with great charm, and undoubtedly served to exemplify the highest quality in the medium for both Girtin and Turner in their early days. Iolo Williams calls him "a suave colourist." His stone and brickwork, in particular, pick up the subtle reflections from trees or nearby surfaces; his figures are completely natural to the scene rather than affecting elegant attitudes.

Rooker was a well-read man, of a retiring character. According to Edward Dayes, he was not as successful as he merited, and, dejected and broken in spirit, "he drooped into eternity" on 3 March 1801, aged 58.

51 THE CHAPEL AT THE GREYFRIARS MONASTERY, WINCHESTER
Watercolor. 9 x 11⅛ inches (23 x 28.5 cm.)
Inscribed: *MR* lower left, and with title on old mount in pencil.
Provenance: Colnaghi 1960.
Exhibited: National Gallery, Washington, 1962, no. 57.

Thomas Hearne (1744–1817)

Hearne, born near Malmesbury in Wiltshire in 1744, worked in London for seven years from 1765 as apprentice to the highly skillful engraver William Woollett, a kindly man who treated him as colleague and friend. From 1771 to 1774 Hearne traveled in the West Indies as draughtsman to the Governor-General, making drawings of ports, harbors, and island scenery. On his return, after preparing his West Indian material for engraving, Hearne determined to devote himself to drawing, and to British topography. In 1777 he began his greatest work, a series of fifty-two drawings which were engraved by his friend William Byrne and published in 1807 as *The Antiquities of Great Britain*.

Hearne was much revered by his contemporaries. Dr. Monro, who owned many of his drawings, considered him "superior to everybody in drawing," and set his young artists to copy and learn from his work; Hearne's drawings had a profound influence especially upon the young Turner. Pilkington called Hearne "the father of all that is good" in British watercolor painting. Hearne's contribution to the art lay not so much in innovation as in restraint and fine judgment in composition. His coloring, when not indeed monochrome, is refined but never insipid: it is a gentle balance of gray, green, and blue. Underpainting in gray tints instead of the conventional India ink gives his architecture delicate sharpness; and his drawings are quickened by lively skies, "with touches of blue appearing through rifts of thin and ragged cloud," which Martin Hardie acclaims as a new feature in topographic art. Something deeper than charm underlies Hearne's art: perhaps that quality which Sir George Beaumont discerned when he wrote of Hearne that "a man of purer integrity does not exist."

Hearne was the intimate friend of Edridge, Dr. Monro, and Farington, whose *Diary* is full of references to him. Hearne died in London on 13 April 1817, and was buried in Bushey churchyard.

52 VIEW FROM SKIDDAW
Watercolor. 7⅜ x 10⅝ inches (18.8 x 27 cm.), on a contemporary mount.
Inscribed: *Hearne* lower left.
Provenance: Sabina Girtin; Tom Girtin; John Baskett 1970.
Exhibited: The Fitzwilliam Museum, Cambridge, 1920, no. 26; Cambridge University Pictorial Arts Society, 1923, no. 74; Graves Art Gallery, Sheffield, *Early Water-colours from the Collection of Thomas Girtin Jnr.*, 1953, no. 63; Leeds City Art Gallery, *Early English Water-colours*, 1958, no. 63; Royal Academy, *The Girtin Collection*, 1962, no. 32.

Francis Wheatley, R.A. (1747–1801)

Wheatley was born in London in 1747, the son of a master tailor. He was awarded a premium at the Society of Arts at fifteen, and had lessons first from Daniel Fournier, engraver, then at Shipley's School, and at the Royal Academy in 1769. While young he worked with Mortimer, and it was probably through him that Wheatley painted his *Cascade Scene* in Vauxhall Gardens, a showpiece with falling water and lighting effects. He was one of Mortimer's assistants in the decoration of the ceiling at Brocket Hall, Hertfordshire, for Lord Melbourne. Wheatley's industry brought him a good income, but not enough for his high style of living. In 1779 he fled to Ireland, leaving numerous creditors unpaid and a reputation tarnished by scandal. J. A. Gresse, a Swiss artist working in London, sued Wheatley for assaulting and ravishing his wife; he won the case, though his claim for £1000 damages diminished by judgment to an award of only five shillings and threepence and costs. With typical fecklessness Wheatley borrowed more money and decamped to Ireland with Mrs. Gresse in the guise of his wife. In Ireland he flourished as a portrait painter, and also made a very large painting of a notable event in Irish history: the Volunteers meeting on College Green, Dublin. Disclosure of the truth about Mrs. Gresse in 1783 made his future in Dublin untenable, and he returned to London. In a short time he was painting another historical scene of a confrontation of troops with the Gordon rioters; this was commissioned by Boydell, for whose *Shakespeare Gallery* Wheatley painted thirteen scenes. In 1792, the year after his election as Royal Academician, he exhibited the first of his fourteen *Cries of London* (only two have been located) which were engraved initially by eminent engravers, and copied ever since in many processes. Of all his work, this series has perpetuated his name as a painter.

Wheatley married in about 1788. The portraits he made of his wife show her to have had an attractive face and elegant poise; he is said to have used her as model for his workaday maidens. During Wheatley's last years, spent in debt and misery from gout, she gave drawing lessons to support him and their four children. Constant borrowing from his fellow-artists ultimately isolated him from any further help from them. Farington, his last and most valuable friend, succeeded in getting a pension from the Academy for the widow after Wheatley's death on 28 June 1801.

A cursory survey of Wheatley's oeuvre shows it to cover general tastes and requirements in English eighteenth-century art. His early landscapes are clearly under the influence of Gainsborough, and his topographical watercolors are much in the manner of Paul Sandby. He could competently compose subjects from sentimental rustics to dignified portraits. His output of watercolors was large, and many have survived with their coloring still fresh and generally unfaded, except for the grays which, as Martin Hardie notes, "become more blue as they recede."

53 DONNYBROOK FAIR, 1782

Watercolor. 12⅝ x 21⅜ inches (32 x 54.2 cm.)
Inscribed: *F. Wheatley / delt: 1782* lower left on cartwheel.
Provenance: Frank T. Sabin 1961.
Exhibited: Victoria, 1971, no. 50, pl. 12.

Scenes of Irish fairs were drawn in many versions by Wheatley. Their actual location, variously entitled Donnybrook or Palmerston fairs, is uncertain, and they are most probably composed from details sketched at different times. He owned several drawings by Wouwermans, of whose manner they are reminiscent. Similar drawings to this are in the collections of the Victoria and Albert Museum, Mrs. D. A. Williamson (London), and Mrs. Cecil Keith (Rusper, Sussex); the Mellon collection also includes another version.

Thomas Malton II (1748–1804)

Malton, born in London, was the eldest son of Thomas Malton, architect, draughtsman, and writer on perspective. He studied for three years under James Gandon and in 1773 was admitted to the Royal Academy schools as an architectural student. His early successes included a premium from the Society of Arts and in 1782 a gold medal from the Academy schools for a "Design for a Theatre"; he later painted scenes for Covent Garden Theatre. From 1783 to 1787 Malton held an evening school for teaching perspective. Among his pupils were Girtin and Turner, each then about twelve years old. His teaching must have been impressive, as Turner, when Professor of Perspective at the Royal Academy, paid tribute to Malton's skill in drawing and instruction. Between 1773 and 1803, Malton exhibited architectural views at the Academy, but on his proposed election as an Associate, was rejected on the grounds that he was "only a draughtsman of buildings, but no architect." Yet as a draughtsman of buildings he excelled, and his drawings, precise in detail and delicate in coloring, have an elegance free from any romanticized embellishment. Malton died in Long Acre, London, on 7 March 1804, "of a putrid fever which at first was nervous."

54 THE ROYAL TERRACE, ADELPHI
Watercolor. 19⅜ x 28¾ inches (49.2 x 73 cm.)
Provenance: John Mitchell & Sons 1963.
Exhibited: Royal Academy, 1774, no. 169.

The Adelphi was a highly imaginative though financially disastrous development of part of the Thames embankment by the Adam brothers. Malton's drawing, exhibited in 1774, shows the recently completed Royal Terrace, a superb series of private houses fronting the river, built over an arched substructure to one consistent pattern, accented by Robert Adam with attenuated pilasters decorated with honeysuckle design ("Warehouses," commented Walpole unkindly, "laced down the front like a soldier's frill on a regimental coat"). Behind the Terrace, the Adelphi buildings extended to subsidiary streets, four of them bearing the Adam brothers' names. No. 8, John Adam Street has been since 1774 the headquarters of the Royal Society of Arts, whose premiums materially helped many young artists. Rowlandson, once supposed to have lived in the Adelphi Tavern, had lodgings in the spacious attics of No. 1, James Street, Adelphi, and died there in 1827. Dr. Thomas Monro, whose name recurs in this catalogue as the friend of Hearne, Alexander, and Edridge and the kindly patron of Girtin, Turner, Cristall,

John and Cornelius Varley, Cotman, Copley Fielding, Hunt, Linnell, De Wint, and many others, lived from 1794 at No. 8, Adelphi Terrace. "Dr. Monro's house is like an Academy in an evening," Farington reported. There he welcomed young artists, giving them access to his pictures and portfolios, letting them sketch from his windows overlooking the Thames, and assisting them with judicious advice.

Much of the Adelphi, including almost the entire south front, was demolished in 1936.

Thomas Daniell, R.A. (1749–1840)

Daniell was born at Kingston-upon-Thames, son of an innkeeper. After serving his apprenticeship to a coach and heraldic painter he was employed in that trade by Charles Catton, R.A., coachpainter to George III. He entered the Royal Academy schools in 1773 and became a landscape painter, exhibiting at the Royal Academy from 1772 to 1824.

In December 1784 Daniell received permission from the East India Company for his nephew William and himself to proceed to Bengal. At that time in India culture was fast following commerce; the demand for artists grew, as did stories of success from artists already there. Thomas Daniell and his nephew journeyed to India via China. Both were endowed with energy, industry, and skill in drawing. They toured extensively in India for eight years. To ensure topographical accuracy in their prospects of places and buildings of interest they used a camera obscura. William kept diaries accounting for their movements during the years 1788–92. They returned to England in 1794 with a vast compilation of graphic information. The sketches they had made formed the basis of many paintings exhibited by both artists in later years. But the work that commanded most public attention was *Oriental Scenery*, published in parts over the years 1795 to 1808; this comprised 144 large aquatinted plates in color, at a cost of £210 to subscribers.

Daniell's achievements brought him high awards of honor: he was elected Royal Academician in 1799, and became a Fellow of the Royal Society, the Asiatic Society, and the Society of Antiquaries. He died in London on 19 March 1840.

55 VIEW OF SOME-CHEON ON FRENCH ISLAND
Watercolor. 21 x 29¾ inches (53.2 x 75.5 cm.)
Inscribed: *View of Some-Cheon on French Island taken from Danes Island, China*, on the old mount.
Provenance: Hamill and Barker, Chicago, 1960.

French Island and Danes Island were the names of two small islands in the Canton River, near the riverside village of Whampoa; that stretch of the river, besides being constantly busy with Chinese craft of all shapes and sizes, was a compulsory anchorage for foreign ships trading to Canton. On Danes Island, European trading firms were permitted to construct light wooden huts or "bankshalls" for repairing ships, depositing stores, and accommodating sailors, while on French Island, William Hickey reported in 1769, "the officers walk or amuse themselves with different games for exercise or pastime. Upon French Island Europeans who die are buried."

John "Warwick" Smith (1749–1831)

Smith was born on 26 July 1749 at Irthington, Cumberland, the son of a gardener whose employer's brother, Captain John Bernard Gilpin, gave him his first drawing lessons and later placed him as pupil to his son, Sawrey Gilpin, R.A. "Warwick" Smith (the sobriquet was derived from his patronage by the second Earl of Warwick, who subsidized his stay in Italy from 1776 to 1781) was a topographical draughtsman whose work is variable in quality, but who enjoyed considerable contemporary reputation for his coloring, which was thought to have introduced a new forcefulness and richness into watercolor art. Ibbetson, his sketching companion on a tour in Wales in 1788, declared that "in tinted drawings no one . . . ever came so near the tint of nature as Mr. John Smith"; and Pyne, among others, acclaimed him as the first to tint watercolor "almost up to the force of oil painting." Smith indeed often painted with full pigments of dark green, yellowish-green, bright blue, and russet-brown, but there was little that was new in his technique. His best work was done during his five years in Italy. The material he collected then supplied him with themes for the rest of his life, so that he often exchanged the nickname "Warwick" for "Italian" Smith; but the powerful Italian spirit became progressively diluted in the studio. Smith made many sketching tours, particularly in Wales and the Lake District. His English and Welsh views are perhaps most attractive when small in size and richly colored, but Turner complained, not unfairly, of the "sameness and manner" of his style. Many of his drawings were engraved for topographical publications, including seventy-two plates for his own *Select Views in Italy* (1792–99). Smith was a member of the Water-colour Society from 1805 to 1823, holding several offices and exhibiting regularly. He died in London on 22 March 1831.

The drawings Smith made on the spot in Italy show him at his best, responding with a new amplitude of style to the strong sunlight, whether it falls (as in the exhibited drawing) over a wide, spectacular view or on deep-shadowed ruins studied almost in close-up as in some of his Roman drawings in the British Museum. Undoubtedly too, he benefited from the companionship in Italy of William Pars and later of Francis Towne, with whom he traveled back through Switzerland in the autumn of 1781. The influence of Towne in particular on both his coloring and style is obvious, although Smith's manner is milder than Towne's, and has none of his idiosyncrasy. In Italy Smith also enjoyed the society of Thomas Jones, whose *Memoirs* contain several references to sketching excursions with "my friend Smith the Landscape painter"; and since nothing is recorded elsewhere about Smith's personality, it is pleasant to glimpse through the *Memoirs* the two friends sketching Vesuvius after "climbing up on all fours," refreshing themselves "with Eggs & Bacon & a flask" or, in Smith's hillside lodgings in Rome, spending "many agreeable Evenings with Song and Dance &c."

56 VILLA MEDICI, ROME

Watercolor. 13¾ x 20¼ inches (34.8 x 51.5 cm.)

Inscribed: 𝒥S (conjoined) lower right, and verso, *Villa Medici at Rome, from the Strada Babourni.*

Provenance: Iolo A. Williams; the family of the late Iolo A. Williams 1970.

There is another version of this drawing in the British Museum (1936–7-4-27), and a drawing of the same view by Thomas Jones, possibly done at the same time, is in the collection of John F. L. Wright, Esq., Norwich.

John Downman, A.R.A. (1750–1824)

Downman, born in Devonshire, was the son of a Quaker attorney. At nineteen he was a pupil in the first year of the newly formed Royal Academy schools, studying under Benjamin West. His exhibits at the Academy ranged from 1770 to 1819, and he was elected Associate of the Royal Academy in 1795. Portrait painting became his immediate profession, his favorite medium being charcoal or pencil, delicately tinted with watercolor. Such portraits were described by a reviewer in the *Morning Post* of 1797 as ". . . very neatly manufactured and the ladies were mightily pleased because he tinted every cheek with a rosy effusion and washed every bosom with a semblance of Olympian dew." His work in landscape is known by two groups only, those in the Victoria and Albert Museum, drawn in England, and others done in Rome, in the collection of Mr. D. L. T. Oppé, London. Excepting slight tints, these are monochrome drawings; for their fresh style Martin Hardie links Downman with Towne as "an innovator with an entirely fresh eye for form and design." Downman moved frequently from London, living and working at Cambridge, Exeter, and Chester; he died at Wrexham, Denbighshire, on 24 December 1824.

57 MRS. IVES OF CATTON, 1780
  Black stub tinted with watercolor. 9 x 7¼ inches (22.7 x 18.2 cm.), oval.
  Inscribed: *J. D. / 1780* center of subject.
  Provenance: Sir Gervaise Beckett, Bt.; Agnew 1965.

  A photograph of a drawing by Downman of a Mrs. Ives of Catton, similarly signed and dated, is in the British Museum. It shows a much older woman; the Mrs. Ives portrayed here is possibly her daughter-in-law.

John Webber, R.A. (1750?–1793)

Webber, the son of a Swiss sculptor, was born in London but was sent abroad for his early artistic education. In Berne he studied under J. L. Aberli, the originator of a picturesque manner of portraying Swiss mountain scenery. Returning to London, Webber studied at the Royal Academy schools. In 1776, through the influence of Dr. Solander, he was appointed official draughtsman on Captain Cook's third voyage. Cook himself emphasized the importance of professional drawings as a complement to scientific records: "Mr. Webber was engaged to embark with me," he wrote, "for the express purpose of supplying the unavoidable imperfections of written accounts." Webber made numerous drawings not only of landscape but also, in Cook's words, "of everything that was curious, both within and without doors." His sketches of natives, their houses, clothing, utensils, and customs add a vivid gloss to Cook's narrative. Webber was an eyewitness of Cook's death, and his painting of it, engraved by Byrne and Bartolozzi, became the standard representation of that tragic event.

On his return to London Webber superintended the engraving of his drawings for the official account of the expedition published by the Admiralty in 1784, although his sketches of native faces and costume inevitably suffered some "Europeanization" in the engravers' hands. Webber himself engraved and published a series of *Views in the South Seas* (1787–92), and exhibited at the Royal Academy several paintings based on the voyage. He was elected Associate of the Royal Academy in 1785, and Royal Academician in 1791. From 1790 his exhibits there included English landscapes. He made several sketching tours in Wales and Derbyshire, delineating the rocky terrain with the same studious, attentive eye that he had bent on less familiar regions. He appears never to have essayed imaginative or deliberately romantic subjects. His draughtsmanship is invariably fine and detailed. His coloring is restrained and delicate: the contemporary comment of Edward Edwards that he is "frequently too gaudy" is difficult to understand.

Webber's particular friends among artists were Farington and Hearne, to each of whom he bequeathed drawings. He died in London on 29 May 1793.

58 LANDSCAPE IN DERBYSHIRE

Pencil and watercolor. 13½ x 18¾ inches (33.6 x 47.7 cm.)
Inscribed: Verso, *3 / Pickerel* in pencil.
Provenance: Iolo A. Williams; Colnaghi 1963.

Webber's friends included the amateur geologist and artist William Day, honorary exhibitor at the Royal Academy from 1782 to 1801. Webber and Day made several sketching tours together, notably in Derbyshire in 1789, in which year this drawing was almost certainly made. Several pairs of drawings by Webber and Day of the same subject are known (one in the Mellon collection), and a drawing by Day of this subject, inscribed "The Pickerell, on the Staffordshire side of Dovedale," is in a private collection. While Day stimulated Webber's interest in geology, his artistic debt to Webber is evident in his own drawings. They had in common a predilection for rugged landscape, and a wish to portray the natural nobility of particular conformations in an accurate rather than a picturesque manner.

John Brown (1752–1787)

Brown was born in Edinburgh in 1752, the son of a goldsmith and watchmaker. He studied in the Edinburgh School of Art under its master, William Delacour, who made a crayon portrait of him (now in the Scottish National Portrait Gallery). At the age of nineteen, in 1771, Brown went to Rome, probably studying there under his fellow-Scot Alexander Runciman. There, too, he came under the stimulating influence of Fuseli, eleven years older than himself, who lived in Rome from 1770 to 1778; they had much in common, including a reverence for Michelangelo and a taste for literature (Brown became fluent in Italian, composed poetry in that language, and wrote *Letters Upon the Poetry and Music of the Italian Opera*, published posthumously). Brown sometimes worked very much in Fuseli's eerie and extravagant manner, particularly in his drawings of Roman women, who have what Iolo Williams calls "a creepily haunting quality." Fuseli's only recorded comment about Brown unfortunately betrays impatience, though possibly only with his companions: "One day, as Fuseli, Northcote and Legat the engraver were walking from Hampstead to London, the two latter gentlemen were extolling the talent of Brown, the Draughtsman, who was so much noticed by Mr. Townley. Fuseli, after listening to the artist's praise, exclaimed 'Well Brown, Brown, we have had enough of Brown; let us now talk of Cipriani who is in Hell!' "

Brown spent "above ten years" in Italy, working for part of the time for Charles Townley and Sir William Young, antiquarians studying Sicilian antiquities; he sent two views of antiquities to the Royal Academy in 1774. He is known to have drawn a portrait of Piranesi, now lost. He returned to Edinburgh in 1781, and was commissioned by the Earl of Buchan to draw portraits of the members of the newly founded Society of Antiquaries in Scotland. Some thirty of these large pencil drawings survive, including a portrait of Runciman. Brown also attracted the patronage of the judge and philosopher Lord Monboddo, and was often a guest at his "Attic suppers." In 1786 Brown left for London, exhibiting at the Royal Academy that year for the second and last time, and again working for Charles Townley. His health, never robust, broke down; he embarked in London for Edinburgh, but became extremely ill on the voyage, and died soon after landing, on 5 September 1787, aged 35.

59 THE GEOGRAPHERS

Pen, ink, and wash. 7⅛ x 10 inches (18 x 25.2 cm.). Verso, pencil sketch of seated man reading a book, semi-back view.

Inscribed: *John Brown Romae* in pencil to right of table, and *61* top right corner.

Provenance: Sir Thomas Lawrence, sold Christie's 17 June 1830, lot 105, bought Knowles; Lady North; Leon Suzor; Faerber & Maison 1965.

Literature: Nicolas Powell, "Brown and the Women of Rome," *Signature*, new series no. 14, 1952, ill. between pp. 42 and 43.

Exhibited: Musée Carnavalet, Paris, *Chefs d'oeuvre des Collections Parisiennes*, 1950, no. 94.

This is one of the eighteen drawings by Brown from the collection of Sir Thomas Lawrence, and in his sale on 17 June 1830 was described as "A group of six students, a large book open before them; on the reverse a portrait of a man reading, in pencil."

John Robert Cozens (1752–1797)

John Robert Cozens was the only son of Alexander Cozens. He is recorded as an exhibitor with the Society of Artists from 1767 to 1771, when he was living with his father in Leicester Street, London. In 1776 he left England for Italy, traveling through Switzerland, where he made a series of drawings under the inspection of Richard Payne Knight, the collector and writer on the picturesque. Thomas Jones mentions in his *Memoirs* that he met Cozens together with William Pars, Jacob More, and Henry Fuseli at the English Coffee House on the first day of his, Jones's, arrival in Rome on 27 November 1776. Payne Knight visited Sicily with Charles Gore and Philip Hackert, and on their return he employed Cozens to make watercolor copies of some of their landscape sketches. On 8 April 1779 Jones records that "little Cozens set off this day for England." In Florence, quite fortuitously, he found the drawings that Alexander Cozens (q.v.) had lost in 1746; he bought them, and gave them to his father on his return to England. Cozens became acquainted, through his father, with the latter's pupil and friend, William Beckford, the author of *Vathek*. On Beckford's third journey to the Continent in 1782 he took John Robert Cozens with him as draughtsman, and was accompanied by an impressive cavalcade comprising a tutor, a physician, a musician, and many other attendants. They traveled to Naples via the Tyrol, Venice, Padua, and Ferrara, reaching their destination by July 1782. Cozens went separately to Rome, arriving in December 1782, and stayed for some nine months. He was on his way home to England by the late autumn of 1783.

For the next nine years he worked in England on commissions for watercolors of the subjects drawn on his travels. The most important of these was a series completed for William Beckford. In some instances, where numerous purchasers were to be found, he made several versions of the same subject. By 1794 Cozens had become incurably insane and had probably not been capable of working two years previous to this. He was confined to the care of Dr. Monro and financial support was successfully sought from the Royal Academy and, through Sir George Beaumont, from Richard Payne Knight, Charles Townley, the Rev. C. M. Cracherode, and Sir Henry Englefield. Beckford did not respond to an appeal, which would seem to imply that he had quarreled with Cozens at an earlier date. The artist died aged 45 in 1797.

60 THE LAKE OF ALBANO AND CASTEL GANDOLFO

Watercolor. 17½ x 25⅜ inches (44.5 x 64.5 cm.)

Provenance: C. Morland Agnew; C. Gerald Agnew; D. Martin Agnew; Agnew 1967.

Literature: *The Studio*, Winter Number 1917–18; C. F. Bell and T. Girtin, *The Drawings and Sketches of John Robert Cozens*, Walpole Society, vol. XXIII, 1935, p. 46, no. 147(v).

Francis Hawcroft in his exhibition catalogue, *Water-colours by John Robert Cozens*, Whitworth Art Gallery, Manchester, and Victoria and Albert Museum, 1971, p. 19, no. 28, lists eight other versions of this subject, which are related to number 14 in the Soane Museum's book of *28 Sketches by J. Cozens of Views in Italy. 1776–78*. One other of these versions, formerly in the possession of Tom Girtin, Esq., is now in the Mellon collection. There are subtle differences in the lighting and atmospheric effects in several of the versions.

61 THE PAYS DE VALAIS, NEAR THE LAKE OF GENEVA
Watercolor. 14 x 20½ inches (35.5 x 52 cm.)
Provenance: Col. H. Littlewood, c.m.g.; Colnaghi 1961.
Literature: C. F. Bell and T. Girtin, *John Robert Cozens*, Walpole Society, vol. XXIII, 1935, p. 29, no. 12 (where six other versions of the composition are listed).
Exhibited: National Gallery, Washington, 1962, no. 23 (ill.); V.M.F.A., Richmond, 1963, no. 65; Colnaghi, 1964–65, and Yale University Art Gallery, 1965, no. 25 (ill.).

Number 15 in the Soane Museum's volume entitled *28 Sketches by J. Cozens of Views in Italy 1776–78* is entitled *Pais* [sic] *de Valais* and is dated Aug. 30 1776 on the mount. On the back are the names of eight patrons who ordered versions of the subject. Six versions are named by Bell and Girtin (*op. cit.*). The Mellon drawing, which was unknown to Bell and Girtin, reappeared at a country-house auction sale in Norfolk some ten years ago.

Francis Hawcroft, in his catalogue of the exhibition of *Water-colours by John Robert Cozens* (Whitworth Art Gallery and Victoria and Albert Museum, 1971), convincingly suggests that the device of the sun's rays breaking through cloud could have been an inspiration derived from a drawing by Alexander Cozens, now in the British Museum (1867–10-12-17).

62 NEAR CHIAVENNA IN THE GRISONS
Watercolor. 16¾ x 24½ inches (42.5 x 62.2 cm.)
Provenance: F. J. C. Holdsworth; C. Morland Agnew; Hugh L. Agnew; Lady Mayer; Agnew 1971.
Literature: C. F. Bell and T. Girtin, *The Drawings and Sketches of John Robert Cozens*, Walpole Society, vol. XXIII, 1935, p. 35, no. 47 (II).
Exhibited: Whitworth Art Gallery, Manchester, *Water-colour Drawings by J. R. Cozens and John Sell Cotman*, 1937; Agnew, *Loan Exhibition of Water-colour Drawings by John Robert Cozens*, 1947, no. 1.

Cozens' monochrome drawing of this subject, in the City Art Gallery, Leeds (Norman D. Lupton bequest), was exhibited at Agnew's, *Water-colours and Drawings from the City Art Gallery, Leeds*, 1960, no. 26.

63 ON THE LAKE OF NEMI
Watercolor. 8⅛ x 11¾ inches (21 x 30 cm.), on early mount.
Provenance: Sir Thomas Barlow, Bt.; Sir Thomas D. Barlow, g.b.e.; Colnaghi 1961.
Literature: C. F. Bell and T. Girtin, *The Drawings and Sketches of John Robert Cozens*, Walpole Society, vol. XXIII, 1935, p. 45, no. 142(c), pl. XIIa.
Exhibited: National Gallery, Washington, 1962, no. 21; V.M.F.A., Richmond, 1963, no. 64; Colnaghi, 1964–65, and Yale University Art Gallery, 1965, no. 83.

Though this drawing is on the same paper and is of the same size as a drawing made on the Arno which dates after 1783, both appear to belong to a series made by the artist on a different kind of paper, some of which are dated 1780.

64 IL PARCO DEGLI' ASTRONI: THE WOODED CRATER BOTTOM, WITH A HUNT IN PROGRESS

Watercolor. 10¼ x 14⅛ inches (26 x 36 cm.), with ⅛ in. gilt border.

Inscribed: Verso *In the Astruni near Naples.*

Provenance: Professor E. Davison Telford; sold Sotheby's 14 March 1962, lot 62; Colnaghi 1962.

Literature: C. F. Bell and T. Girtin, *The Drawings and Sketches of John Robert Cozens*, Walpole Society, vol. XXIII, 1935, pp. 65–67, nos. 311–318; and cf. pl. XXIVb for one of the annotated sketches.

Bell and Girtin identify five sketches of this subject from the Beckford books (IV, 24–28), but state that the drawings from them, two of which they trace as far as the C. S. Bale sale of 1881, have since disappeared. This drawing appeared at auction in 1962.

The Parco degli' Astroni, the crater of an extinct volcano near Naples, was used in the eighteenth century for royal hunts. Miss Berry witnessed one of these *battues* in 1784, and stated that "a more barbarous amusement was never practised by the savages of America."

John Raphael Smith (1752–1812)

Smith was born at Derby, the son of Thomas Smith, a landscape painter known as "Smith of Derby." Either through disinclination or indolence, Smith did not at first follow the family bent for art, and was apprenticed to a linen-draper. At sixteen he was a shopman in London, practicing miniature painting in his leisure time. He tried his hand at engraving and discovered his métier, mezzotinting. He developed his skill at this rapidly, while at the same time selling fineries to ladies from a shop he now owned in the Strand. Orders mounted for his plates; and to meet the demand, he had to take premises for the equipment required, and to house his assistants and apprentices. Turner and Girtin at one time were employed coloring prints for him, and James and William Ward and Peter De Wint counted among his pupils. Nearly four hundred of Smith's mezzotints are recorded, most being of the highest quality from paintings by Reynolds, Romney, and other well-known painters. He prospered especially from his companionship with Morland, from whose paintings he produced prints in such quantity that his income was ten times that of the painter. Both men enjoyed together the boisterous life of the alehouse and its attendant sports, to a stage of dissipation; but, predictably, a cleft in the friendship parted them for good. With the troubles following the French Revolution, Smith's business declined, and as his publishing business shrank he turned to portrait drawings in pastel, which proved financially successful; he is said to have done forty a week at two guineas a time.

Smith exhibited frequently in mezzotint, crayon, and oil painting, contributing in these media regularly at the Royal Academy from 1779 to 1805. In character he was genial, hard-working, and shrewd; a bulky man with tough physique. His biographer, Julia Frankau, is both laudatory and censorious of him, applauding his success in spite of early hardships, but deploring his neglect of ambition for the full use of his talents which "lay choked with the refuse of his dissipations." How he might have progressed without these impediments is conjectural, as few engravers could equal his skill in mezzotint or the overall quality he maintained throughout. He died at Doncaster on 2 March 1812, in his sixtieth year.

65 THE CHARMER

Black chalk and stump heightened with white on prepared paper. 14¼ x 10½ inches (36.2 x 26.7 cm.)
Provenance: Agnew 1962.
Exhibited: Colnaghi, 1964–65, and Yale University Art Gallery, 1965, no. 31.

Thomas Stothard, R. A. (1755–1834)

Stothard was born on 17 August 1755, the son of a Covent Garden innkeeper. When he was fifteen his father died, leaving him a legacy. For a short time he was apprenticed to a pattern draughtsman for brocaded silks. In 1788 he entered the Royal Academy schools, lodging with Samuel Shelley, later a successful miniaturist. Book illustration became Stothard's chief occupation in life, and several thousands of his designs were engraved. His oil paintings, except for ceiling decorations, done at Burleigh House for the Marquis of Exeter, and at the Advocates' Library in Edinburgh, were for the most part on a small scale. These when exhibited at the Royal Academy, although admired, did not have sufficient impact to ensure widespread popularity and elevate him to fame. He is sometimes termed "history painter," but his best "history" piece was the Wellington Shield, and it is evident from this that Stothard was a designer by instinct. The shield was a gift to the Duke of Wellington from bankers and merchants, and Stothard's design for it established his reputation with all the leading gold- and silversmiths.

Stothard exhibited ninety times at the Royal Academy from 1778 to 1834; he was elected Associate of the Royal Academy in 1791 and full Academician in 1794. He also held the post of Librarian there from 1814 to 1834. Some of his work is reminiscent of Blake's. They had been friends for about thirty years when a double-dealing action by R. H. Cromek, an engraver and publisher, concerning their respective designs for the "Canterbury Tales," created a breach between them that never healed.

Stothard's life was saddened many times, especially by bereavements in his family and circle of friends, but he was fortified against despair by his gentle and placid nature. These qualities in his character are reflected in his work, notably the drawings, which, although full of charm and grace, are inventive rather than imaginative. James Smetham called him "the Quaker of art" and believed that "the Charles Lamb of Quakerness with all its doveiness was embodied in his work." He suffered from serious deafness during his last years, and died in London on 27 April 1834, aged nearly 80.

66 DESIGN FOR A SILVER CHALICE

Sepia. 15⅜ x 16¾ inches (39 x 42.6 cm.)
Provenance: Colnaghi 1966.

This chalice was executed by the goldsmiths Rundell and Bridge. There is an earlier, smaller version of the design in the British Museum (L.B.116).

67 A DISTANT VIEW OF EDINBURGH, 1809

Pencil and watercolor. 8⅜ x 16⅜ inches (21.2 x 41.5 cm.)
Inscribed: *1809 / Edinburgh / Stothard / 23 July / 1809,* on old mount.
Provenance: Colnaghi 1962.

Stothard's landscape drawings are rare. This view was presumably made when he was staying in Edinburgh in 1822 to paint the Cupola of the Hall at the Advocates' Library.

Samuel Howitt (1756–1822)

Howitt, born in 1756, was a member of an old Nottinghamshire Quaker family. An enthusiastic sportsman, he was a self-taught artist who turned professional when financial difficulties forced him to earn a living. His earliest exhibits, in 1783 at the Incorporated Society of Artists, were three "stained drawings" of hunting scenes; he continued to exhibit occasionally at the Royal Academy and elsewhere until 1815. His talent for drawing animals, from hares and deer to exotic species studied from life in menageries, led to many commissions to illustrate sporting and zoological books, including *Miscellaneous Etchings of Animals* (1803), *Oriental Field Sports* (1807), Aesop's *Fables* (1811), and *The British Sportsman* (1812). He was an accomplished etcher, and occasionally painted in oils.

Howitt was a friend of Rowlandson, whose sister Elizabeth he married on 2 October 1779. His early watercolors are very close to Rowlandson's in style and coloring. Though his work seldom attains Rowlandson's superb vivacity (and hardly attempts Rowlandson's social comment) there is nevertheless always an air of briskness about Howitt's drawings: his animals are credibly poised to pounce, or fly, or slink away; his hunts proceed apace and his coaches bowl through fresh air. Howitt died in London in 1822.

68 A COACH PASSING THROUGH CHIPPENHAM

Pen, gray ink, and watercolor. 6⅛ x 19¾ inches (15.5 x 50.5 cm.)
Provenance: Anonymous owner, sold Christie's 14 October 1969, lot 77 (ill.); John Baskett 1969.
Exhibited: Victoria, 1971, no. 21.

Thomas Rowlandson (1757–1827)

Rowlandson was born in Old Jewry, London, on 14 July 1757,* the son of a textile merchant. His father was declared bankrupt in 1759, and Rowlandson was cared for by a paternal uncle for five years and thereafter by the uncle's widow. He went to Dr. Barvis' reputable school, and joined the Royal Academy schools when fifteen. His indulgent aunt sent him to Paris for some weeks during this period. At the Academy schools he met Jack Bannister who, although later a renowned comedian, remained one of Rowlandson's more sober-minded friends. He exhibited fairly regularly at the Academy from 1775 to 1787, his first exhibit being a religious subject, *Dalilah payeth Sampson a visit while in Prison in Gaza*. Henry Wigstead, a Bow Street magistrate, found in Rowlandson a friendly traveling companion and an artist who could vivify Wigstead's own ideas on subjects to caricature. Several drawings exhibited at the Academy under Wigstead's name were unquestionably by his friend, and recognized as such by reviewers.

Rowlandson's most important compositions were made in and about his early thirties, and included *Vauxhall Gardens*, shown at the Royal Academy in 1784 and extolled by the King and the critics alike. It was splendidly engraved, and published the following year, and is said to have inspired Debucourt's famous print *Promenade de la Galerie du Palais Royal* which appeared two years later in France. Rowlandson had by then cultivated his gift of drawing to its apex, and thereafter his facility with pen and color rarely faltered, even if his choice of subjects grew more commonplace. His memory retained incidents and situations to be drawn later, and the humor or pathos involved, more often than not, depended upon a crucial pen-stroke. He was a man endowed with mental and physical vigor, and with his companions in art, J. Raphael Smith, Morland, and Gillray, lived a raucous life, gambling and hard-drinking with the usual ancillary activities. He squandered a large legacy from his aunt, sank to poverty before he was forty, but emerged still young enough to recoup his self-respect. A fortunate friendship with Mathew Mitchell, a genial, corpulent banker, provided him with a generous companion who paid for their jaunts to the West Country and the Continent. From that time forward, he worked hard making drawings for book illustrations, exhibitions, satires, and etchings. His long association with the fine-art publisher Rudolph Ackermann had begun in the 1790's. He worked with Augustus Pugin on the plates for *The Microcosm of London*, 1808–11; his *Three Tours of Doctor Syntax* appeared from 1812 to 1821; *The English Dance of Death* from 1814 to 1816; and *The Dance of Life* in 1817. He admitted to feeling ashamed of the mass of etchings which he made for Thomas Tegg: they were feeble and crude but popular, and sold well.

In 1818 Rowlandson made a will leaving everything to a Miss Betsy Winter, described as "now living with me." He died after an illness of two years on 21 April 1827, and was buried in St. Paul's, Covent Garden.

In all, Rowlandson stands unique among artists in leaving behind a serio-comic archive of his period. Notables usually seen in grand portraits are recognized in less reputable sur-

---

* On his admission to the Royal Academy schools on 6 November 1772, Rowlandson stated his age as "15 on 14th July last." The year of his birth has often been given as 1756.

roundings; limbs and features distorted with gout are meant to reflect gluttony, not cruel fun; cuckolds, his most repetitive theme, obviously deserve the deceitfulness of their wives.

69 A REVIEW IN THE MARKET PLACE, WINCHESTER

Pen and watercolor. 11⅜ x 17½ inches (28.7 x 44.5 cm.), on contemporary mount.

Provenance: Gilbert Davis (Lugt 757a); Colnaghi 1961.

Exhibited: National Gallery, Washington, 1962, no. 62; V.M.F.A., Richmond, 1963, no. 432.

70 A WORN-OUT DEBAUCHER

Watercolor. 11¾ x 7¾ inches (29.9 x 19.7 cm.)

Inscribed: *A worn-out Debaucher* in pencil lower center.

Provenance: T. E. Lowinsky (Lugt 2420a); Justin Lowinsky; Colnaghi 1963.

71 OLD VAUXHALL GARDENS

Pen and ink and watercolor. 13 x 18⅛ inches (33 x 46 cm.)

Provenance: L. S. Delatigny (Lugt 1768a); Sir William Augustus Frazer, Bt.; Leggatt Bros. 1963.

Literature: Bernard Falk, *Thomas Rowlandson*, 1949, p. 78; Martin Hardie, I, p. 212, pl. 213.

Exhibited: Royal Institute of Painters in Water-colours, *Works of English Humorists in Art*, 1899, no. 32; V.M.F.A., Richmond, 1963, no. 492; Victoria, 1971, no. 32, pl. 6.

Engraved: In aquatint by R. Pollard and F. Jukes, 28 June 1785.

This drawing appears to be the earliest of four known versions (one in oils); the one in the Victoria and Albert Museum was probably that shown in the Royal Academy exhibition of 1784. Among the well-known figures of the day portrayed are (in the supper box beneath the musicians) Dr. Johnson, Boswell, Mrs. Thrale, and Oliver Goldsmith; Mrs. Weichsel is singing in the orchestra, and standing in the foreground are the Prince of Wales, the actress Mrs. Robinson and her husband, the Duchess of Devonshire, Lady Duncannon, Captain Topham, Admiral Paisley, James Perry, Parson Bate Dudley, Mrs. Hartley, and others.

72 A HORSE SALE AT HOPKINS' REPOSITORY, BARBICAN

Watercolor. 10⅝ x 15¾ inches (27 x 40 cm.)

Provenance: Gilbert Davis (Lugt 757a); the late Sir Eldred Hitchcock, sold Sotheby's 24 February 1960, lot 18; Colnaghi 1960.

Exhibited: National Gallery, Washington, 1962, no. 65; V.M.F.A., Richmond, 1963, no. 428; Victoria, 1971, no. 33.

The Barbican, a street in the City of London which runs between Aldersgate Street and Golden Lane, derived its name from a watchtower or barbican of the ancient wall which formed an outwork in the street.

Watercolor. 11 x 16½ inches (28 x 42 cm.), on contemporary mount.

Inscribed: *Rowlandson 1798* lower right.

Provenance: George, 5th Duke of Gordon; Elizabeth, Duchess of Gordon; The Brodie of Brodie; Agnew 1962.

Exhibited: V.M.F.A., Richmond, 1963, no. 491; Colnaghi, 1964–65, and Yale University Art Gallery, 1965, no. 27 (ill.)

William Blake (1757–1827)

The poet and painter William Blake was born on 28 November 1757 in London, the son of a hosier. He entered Henry Pars's drawing school in the Strand in 1767 but his basic training was as an engraver. He was apprenticed to James Basire from 1772 to 1779, in part working in Westminster Abbey copying medieval tombs for antiquarian publications. He entered the Royal Academy schools in 1779, again to study engraving, but objected to the routine life-studies and copying from antique casts.

In 1780 Blake exhibited for the first time at the Royal Academy: a watercolor of *The Death of Earl Goodwin*. This, like many of his early works, was in the manner of the neoclassical history paintings of Benjamin West and Gavin Hamilton, but the same year he also engraved the first state of the already completely personal *Dance of Albion* (or *Glad Day*, its traditional title). Equally personal are many of the poems published as *Poetical Sketches* in 1783 but dating from his twelfth to twentieth years, and it was in fact in his poetry that he was at his most creative in his early years.

Blake married Catherine Butcher in 1782 and in 1784 set up a printshop with James Parker, but this partnership broke up the following year. He continued to exhibit sporadically at the Royal Academy in 1784 and 1785, and later in 1799, 1800, and 1808.

The first important example of Blake's series of illuminated books, done in a unique technique which printed both the text and the outline of the design, was *Songs of Innocence*, although the previous year he had already tried it out in the tiny *There Is No Natural Religion* and *All Religions Are One*. At about the same time, however, he was still illustrating his first symbolic poem, *Tiriel*, with separate drawings in pen and wash. In 1790 he moved to Lambeth and in the "Lambeth Books" of the next five years he developed this process, at the same time increasing the forcefulness of his designs. Finally, in *Urizen* of 1794, he dropped his practice of coloring his designs individually by hand in watercolor in favor of printing the colors in heavy pigments, a process which he used again on a larger scale in his color prints of 1795. For a few years from 1794, copies of others of his books were color-printed in the same way, although after about 1800, as with his later poems *Milton* and *Jerusalem*, he returned to using watercolor.

The later 1790's were perhaps a period of marking time. Bogged down in the never-completed manuscript of *Vala* or *The Four Zoas*, he produced no new illuminated books, and his chief works were the 537 watercolor illustrations to Edward Young's *Night Thoughts* and

54

the 116 similar illustrations to Gray's *Poems*, the latter being commissioned by his friend the sculptor John Flaxman in 1797. About 1799 he received his first commission from his most important patron, the minor civil servant Thomas Butts. This was for a series of small paintings in tempera of subjects from the Bible which were followed over the next fifteen years by watercolors of similar subjects; replicas of the illustrations to Milton he painted for the Rev. Joseph Thomas from 1801 onwards, and the first series of watercolor illustrations to the *Book of Job*.

From 1800 to 1803 the patronage of William Hayley led him to live at Felpham near Chichester, the only years he lived away from London. Despite Hayley's good intentions Blake felt himself to be deflected from his true purposes by Hayley's mundane commissions to decorate his library, illustrate his various publications, and paint miniatures, and after three years he rebelled and returned to London.

In 1805 Blake undertook to illustrate Robert Blair's *The Grave* but, like all Blake's efforts to achieve a wider market through his illustrations, the project ended in disaster. R. H. Cromek, the publisher, entrusted the engraving of the designs, the most profitable part of the enterprise, to the fashionable Louis Schiavonetti, leading to bitter accusations of ill-faith. Blake also accused Cromek of stealing his idea of painting and then engraving *The Canterbury Pilgrims* and passing it on to Thomas Stothard, ending Blake's long-standing friendship with that artist.

These and other frustrations led in 1809 to Blake's mounting his only one-man exhibition. This included *The Canterbury Pilgrims* as well as other paintings in tempera and watercolor. The exhibition, though prolonged into the following year, was a complete failure. Records of the following eight years of Blake's life are very shadowy: he continued to work on *Milton* and *Jerusalem* and to paint watercolor illustrations to Milton and other works. In 1812 he exhibited as a member at the breakaway society of Associated Painters in Water-colours. At one point during this period he was reduced to making engravings for domestic pottery for Wedgwood's catalogue, and in 1821 or 1822 he was forced to sell his collection of prints. In 1818, however, he made the acquaintance of the young painter John Linnell, and of a group of young artists calling themselves "The Ancients," including Samuel Palmer, George Richmond, and Edward Calvert. In his last years Linnell replaced Butts as Blake's chief patron, paying him what in effect amounted to a regular wage in return for his work, which included a duplicate series of Job watercolors and illustrations to Dante's *Divine Comedy*. Both series were to be engraved, though the latter was left unfinished at Blake's death on 12 August 1827, as was a series of illustrations to Bunyan's *Pilgrim's Progress* and an illustrated manuscript of the Old Testament. Linnell had also introduced Blake to his credulous and superstitious former teacher, the landscape watercolorist John Varley, for whom, mainly in 1819, Blake drew the "Visionary Heads," studies of presumed visions of *The Ghost of a Flea*, *The Man who built the Pyramids*, and many historical and biblical visitants.

74 TIRIEL SUPPORTING THE SWOONING MYRATANA AND ADDRESSING THREE OF HIS SONS

Pen and gray ink, gray wash. 7½ x 10¾ inches (19 x 27.3 cm.)

Provenance: Mrs. Blake; Frederick Tatham; Joseph Hogarth, sold Southgate's 8 June

1854, lot 643; Elhanan Bicknell, sold Christie's 1 May 1863, lot 387; James Leathart; P. W. Leathart; Mrs. Leathart; Sotheby's 19 May 1958, lot 13; Agnew; Gwen, Lady Melchett, sold Christie's 9 November 1971, lot 72; John Baskett 1971.

Literature: Gilchrist, *Life of William Blake*, 1863, vol. II, p. 254; Martin Butlin, "The Bicentenary of William Blake," *Burlington Magazine*, vol. C, pp. 40–44, fig. 2 on p. 45; G. E. Bentley, Jr., *William Blake: Tiriel*, 1967, pp. 30–33, pl. 1; Kathleen Raine, *Blake and Tradition*, 1968, I, p. 37; Kathleen Raine, *William Blake*, 1971, p. 38, fig. 38.

Exhibited: Carfax Galleries, *Blake Exhibition*, 1906, no. 76a; British Museum, *William Blake and His Circle*, 1957, no. 12(6); Newcastle, Laing Art Gallery and Museum, *The Leathart Collection*, 1968, no. 6.

This is the first of twelve (now widely scattered) designs for a dramatic poem, *Tiriel*, written before 1789, which is probably Blake's earliest illuminated narrative. Blake's attempt to link text and design in this work may have led him to create his books in illuminated printing so that the two might be published as a unit. *Tiriel* is a somber and tortured work concerning the abuse of power and the madness and destruction which result from it. Analogies may be found with *King Lear*, Sophocles' *Oedipus at Colonus*, and the story of Joseph in Genesis; there are themes which are similar to those in the writings of Swedenborg, Rousseau, and Mary Wollstonecraft. The costumes and the architecture in this drawing reveal Blake's neoclassical interests. This design illustrates lines 19–20 of the text: "The aged man raisd up his right hand to the heavens[;] his left supported Myratana." The man with a crown is Heuxos, the eldest son of Tiriel and Myratana, who rebelled with his brothers and who took Tiriel's title of "king of the west."

75 "MIDST THE TIDE / TWO ANGEL FORMS WERE SEEN TO GLIDE"

Watercolor, with printed text inlaid off-center. About 16⅖ x 12½ inches (42 x 32 cm.). Verso, in each case: watercolor, with page inlaid.

Provenance: John and Ann Flaxman; sold Christie's 1 July 1828, lot 85; William Clarke(?); William Beckford; 10th Duke of Hamilton and successors, to 1966.

Literature: Gilchrist, *Life of William Blake*, 1863, II, p. 255; H. J. C. Grierson, *William Blake's Designs for Gray's Poems*, 1922; Irene Tayler, *Blake's Illustrations to the Poems of Gray*, 1971; Sir Geoffrey Keynes, catalogue of the exhibition at the Tate Gallery, 1971.

Exhibited: Tate Gallery, *William Blake's Water-Colour Designs for the Poems of Thomas Gray*, 1971.

The data above apply equally to numbers 76 and 77.

Within two years, 1796–97, Blake produced 537 watercolor designs for the *Night Thoughts* of Edward Young, and went on directly to make 116 pages of watercolor designs for Gray's *Poems*. In both cases he used a printed text (here the 1790 edition of Gray's *Poems* published by J. Murray), trimmed off the margins, and inlaid each page in a window cut off-center from a large sheet of Whatman drawing paper. It seems likely that the designs for Gray were completed early in 1798. The work was presented to Mrs.

Flaxman, the wife of the sculptor. The series was purchased as a unit for the Mellon collection in 1966.

The titles for these watercolors (nos. 75–77) are given as Blake wrote them in the lists of subjects for each poem. In this design Selima, Horace Walpole's cat, celebrated in Gray's *Ode on the Death of a Favourite Cat Drowned in a Tub of Gold Fishes*, has been transformed by Blake in a satiric portrayal of woman's frailty and vanity. He radically changed the tone and scene of Gray's poem and reflected his own ideas of sexuality, evil, and regeneration. Blake's illustrations to this poem were consistently the most successful of all his designs for Gray.

76 "YET SEE HOW ALL AROUND THEM WAIT / THE VULTURES OF THE MIND"

After five very gentle illustrations to Gray's *Ode on a Distant Prospect of Eton College*, Blake shows the children (including two girls) playing, "regardless of their doom," while monstrous specters representing Jealousy, Gluttony, Anger, Avarice, Despair, Flattery, Ambition, Scorn, and Infamy descend on them.

77 "HYPERION'S MARCH THEY SPY & GLITTERING SHAFTS OF WAR"

A brilliant, golden vision of Hyperion, the Bowman, seated in a circle fringed with the shafts of war which are also the rays of the sun (imagination and poetry) dispelling the darkness of night (and the evils of materialism): *The Progress of Poesy. A Pindaric Ode*, II, i, 12.

78 "PRONE ON THE LOWLY GRAVE—SHE DROPS"

Pen and gray ink and watercolor. 6⅛ x 8¼ inches (15.5 x 21 cm.), on contemporary bordered mount which is inscribed: *W. Blake. del* and *Prone on the lowly grave—she drops— / Clings yet more closely to the senseless turf / Nor heeds the passenger who looks that way.*

Provenance: Joseph Hogarth; sold Southgate's 7 June 1854, lot 237; H. Palser; J. F. Hall; Carfax; Louisa Salaman; Euston Bishop, sold Sotheby's 19 May 1958, lot 11; Gwen, Lady Melchett, sold Christie's 9 November 1971, lot 74; John Baskett 1971.

Literature: A. G. B. Russell, *The Engravings of William Blake*, 1912, p. 129; G. L. Keynes, *Bibliography of William Blake*, 1921, p. 220; G. E. Bentley, Jr., *Blake Records*, 1969, pp. 166–67, pl. XVIII.

Exhibited: Burlington Fine Arts Club, *Exhibition of the Works of William Blake*, 1876, no. 5.

In 1805 R. H. Cromek commissioned Blake to make forty drawings for Robert Blair's poem *The Grave* and proposed to have twenty of them engraved. Only twelve plates were included in the volume which was published in 1808. Blake expected to do the engraving also, but Cromek assigned this to Schiavonetti, which made Blake feel that he had been treated dishonestly and that his work had been spoiled. Nevertheless, the plates represent some of Blake's finest creations and became his best-known designs. John Flaxman, the sculptor and Blake's friend, in a letter to William Hayley, 18 October

1805 (the manuscript is in The Pierpont Morgan Library), wrote concerning the project: ". . . several Members of the Royal Academy have been highly pleased with the specimens and mean to encourage the work, I have seen several compositions, the most Striking are, The Gambols of Ghosts . . . A widow embracing the turf which covers her husband's grave—Wicked Strong man dying—the Good Old Man's Soul recieved by Angels." The design of the "widow embracing the turf" was not engraved. The lines quoted on the mount are adapted from lines 77–78 and 83–84 of Blair's poem.

79 THE WISE AND FOOLISH VIRGINS

Watercolor. 16½ x 13½ inches (42 x 34.25 cm.)

Exhibited: National Gallery, Washington, 1962, no. 4; V.M.F.A., Richmond, 1963, no. 387; Colnaghi, 1964–65, and Yale University Art Gallery, 1965, no. 1 (frontispiece).

One of six versions of the same subject. The first, painted in 1805 for Blake's patron Thomas Butts, is now in the Metropolitan Museum. The second, done for John Linnell in 1822, is in the Fitzwilliam Museum, Cambridge, and is most closely connected with the watercolor in the Mellon collection. The other versions, two of which may be copies, are later. The subject is taken from Matthew xxv.1–9. The five wise virgins stand holding their lamps and tell the foolish ones to buy oil from "them that sell." The angel with a trumpet announces the approach of the bridegroom.

Julius Caesar Ibbetson (1759–1817)

Ibbetson was born at Farnley Moor, near Leeds, on 29 December 1759, the son of a clothier. After a brief apprenticeship to a ship painter in Hull, and some commissions to paint scenery for the Hull and York Theatres, he went to London and found work with a picture cleaner. Chance took him to Benjamin West's house, where (he later recounted) "for the first time he saw pictures which excited in him a feeling which affected his *very toes.*" For years he earned a very meager living selling his own work to dealers, whom he termed "the old-clothes-men of the arts." He first exhibited at the Royal Academy in 1785, and slowly began to attract patrons. In 1788 he was appointed draughtsman to Cathcart's embassy to China, but returned from Java on Cathcart's death. He made several sketching tours in Wales, one with John "Warwick" Smith. His output was about equally divided between oils and watercolors; his subjects included animal and sporting pictures, landscapes, and portraits. In 1803 he published *An Accidence or Gamut of Painting in Oil and Water-colour,* a treatise which David Wilkie, among others, found extraordinarily useful. Ibbetson whimsically announced that his next publication would be entitled *Humbuggologia,* a treatise on the frauds and pretensions of picture cleaners and dealers. After many financial and domestic troubles he moved to Troutbeck, in the Lake District, and later to Masham, in Yorkshire, where he died on 13 October 1817.

Ibbetson's work in watercolor combines delicate coloring and vigorous subject matter in a very individual manner. His palette was influenced by his early sketching companion John "Warwick" Smith: "in tinted drawings," he declared, "no one . . . can come so near the tint of nature as Mr. Smith." Ibbetson's figure groups—skaters, gypsies, miners, sailors carousing, or coach travelers hurtling over rough roads—are charmingly colored, but drawn with an element of gusto which aligns him with Rowlandson and De Loutherbourg rather than with portrayers of a more elegant contemporary scene; and because he liked to observe people at work, his drawings often have considerable documentary importance. If his work is of uneven quality, Ibbetson himself was grateful for "Genius sometimes lighting me along wth a faint glimmering of his Torch."

80 THE SAILOR'S FAREWELL

Watercolor. 11⅝ x 15⅝ inches (29.6 x 39.7 cm.)
Inscribed: *J. C. Ibbetson 1801* lower right.
Provenance: Sir William Drake (Lugt 736); P. Dangar, sold Christie's 9 November 1971, lot 55; John Baskett 1971.
Literature: Rotha Mary Clay, *Julius Caesar Ibbetson*, 1948, p. 46.
Exhibited: Burlington Fine Arts Club, 1871, no. 126.
Engraved: By Brown in 1804.

A drawing of the same size, *The Sailor's Return Home*, dated 1795, is in the Victoria and Albert Museum (448).

Edward Francis Burney (1760–1848)

Burney was born of a good family near Worcester in September 1760. At the age of sixteen he was sent to study in London and was admitted to the Royal Academy schools, where he gained the friendship of Sir Joshua Reynolds. He exhibited nineteen pictures, mostly portraits, at the Academy between 1780 and 1803. One of his best portraits, painted in 1782, is of his cousin Fanny Burney, who later became Madame d'Arblay. The picture was engraved and used as a frontispiece to her works. Iolo Williams describes Burney's drawings as "precise and neat, but quite without Stothard's innocent charm," and as "cynically witty rather than humorous." His book illustrations were popular, and his clever designs were inlaid in workboxes and other feminine trifles. Burney died in London in December 1848, in his eighty-ninth year.

81 THE TRIUMPH OF MUSIC

Watercolor. 12⅛ x 18⅛ inches (30.7 x 46 cm.)
Provenance: Anonymous owner, sold Christie's 22 June 1962, lot 31; Colnaghi 1962.
Exhibited: V.M.F.A., Richmond, 1963, no. 434; Colnaghi, 1964–65, and Yale University Art Gallery, 1965, no. 30.

Burney made several large satirical drawings in this vein. The Victoria and Albert Museum possesses a watercolor crowded with figures called *An Elegant Establishment for Young Ladies*, and another of the same sort entitled *The Waltz*. A preliminary study for *The Triumph of Music* is in the British Museum.

Edward Dayes (1763–1804)

Dayes was born on 6 August 1763, presumably in London. He worked under William Pether, mezzotinter and miniaturist, until he was seventeen, when he entered the Royal Academy schools. He exhibited at the Academy from the age of twenty-three up to the year he died. Occasionally he painted miniatures and engraved in mezzotint, but his main activity was painting in watercolors. Many of his topographical views were engraved, especially those of antiquarian remains made for the heightened interest in that subject in the eighteenth century. In his major engraved compositions, *The Royal Procession to St. Paul's on the Thanksgiving for the King's Recovery in 1789* and *Buckingham House, St. James's Park* (the drawing for this is in the Victoria and Albert Museum, no. 1756–1871), Dayes shows his skill in drawing an assembly of elegant figures. He became Designer to the Duke of York, and published several books on his excursions in England and on instruction in drawing; he was a teacher of drawing whose most notable pupil was Girtin.

The early drawings of Girtin and Turner show a close affinity to the methods and coloring of Dayes. The two younger artists colored outline etchings by Dayes of regimental costume, some of which are in the Mellon collection.

Dayes's comments on some of his contemporaries, published posthumously, are rather bitter, and his end by suicide in May 1804 reflects his disturbed mind.

82 QUEEN SQUARE

Watercolor. 17¼ x 23½ inches (43.7 x 60 cm.), including contemporary border of 1¼ inches.

Inscribed: E. Dayes / *1786* lower left.
Provenance: Agnew 1968.
Exhibited: Royal Academy, Annual Exhibition, 1787, no. 582.
Engraved: In aquatint by Dodd and Pollard, 1 July 1789, one of a set of four London squares; the others were Bloomsbury, Grosvenor, and Hanover.

William Alexander (1767–1816)

Alexander was born in Maidstone, Kent, on 10 April 1767. His father, a coach painter, brought him to London when he was fifteen, to study first under William Pars, then under J. C. Ibbetson, and later at the Royal Academy schools. Ibbetson recommended Alexander to Lord Macartney as a draughtsman to accompany the party sent to establish an embassy in China. During this expedition, lasting from 1792 to 1794, Alexander made many drawings, some of which were later engraved for Sir George Staunton's handsome account of the whole operation, and others for Alexander's own books of Chinese views and characters. His companion in Peking was Thomas Hickey, the Irish painter; both men were allowed freedom to sketch only when Lord Macartney was in Peking. If he was absent, they were confined to a house with a high wall around it.

On Alexander's return to England he exhibited views of China at the Royal Academy from 1795 to 1800. He held the post of drawing-master at the Royal Military College at Great Marlow from 1802 to 1808. This provided a fair basis for his living, but like David Cox at a later date, he found certain customs in the military establishment irksome to a civilian.

Alexander had built up a connection within the British Museum over some years, and in 1808 was appointed as the first Keeper of Prints and Drawings, a position he retained up to his death from brain fever at Maidstone on 23 July 1816. He had an amiable manner and charitable disposition; his keen intellect can be observed in his many and varied activities, from his early drawings in China to his later delicate monochromes of churches and crosses. An amusing self-portrait drawing in the British Museum shows him in a uniform jacket, hatless, with a patch over his right eye which gives him a slightly piratical appearance.

83 CITY OF LIN-TSIN, SHANTUNG WITH A VIEW OF THE GRAND CANAL

Watercolor. 11¼ x 17⅜ inches (28.5 x 44 cm.)

Inscribed: *W. Alexander 95* in ink lower right, and verso *Lin Tsin—Grand Canal* in pencil on right-hand side.

Provenance: Direct descendants of the artist's family; Spink 1964.

Literature: Sir George Staunton, *An Authentic Account of the Earl of Macartney's Embassy from the King of Great Britain to the Emperor of China*, 1797, pl. 33, engraved by William Byrne.

84 THE DINNER IN MOTE PARK, MAIDSTONE AFTER THE ROYAL REVIEW OF THE KENTISH VOLUNTEERS ON 1ST AUGUST 1799

Pencil and watercolor. 14½ x 21⅞ inches (37 x 55.5 cm.), damaged at edges.

Provenance: Edward Hughes; S. R. Hughes-Smith; Agnew 1971.

Engraved: In aquatint by Alexander, published 1 March 1800.

This cheerful scene on a fine summer's day, in the grounds of a country house in Kent, illustrates one aspect of England at war. The Earl of Romney, Lord Lieutenant of Kent, is giving a vast open-air banquet in honor of over 5,000 volunteers for Kentish regiments of militia to fight against Napoleon. King George III and Queen Charlotte, having reviewed the Volunteers, are dining in the royal marquee, while the Volunteers, seated at 91 tables, are working their way through 60 lambs, 700 fowls, 300 hams, 300 tongues, 1100 dishes of boiled beef, roast beef, veal, meat pies and fruit pies, 7 pipes of wine, and 16 butts of beer. The spectators include the figure of the artist, on the bank toward the right-hand corner. Alexander exhibited another version of the drawing at the Royal Academy in 1800. His engraving of the subject (one guinea plain, two guineas colored) had both decorative and patriotic appeal, and was at once popular.

Joshua Cristall (1767 or 1769 – 1847)

Cristall, the son of a Scottish sea captain, was born in 1767 or 1769 either in London or in his mother's county, Cornwall. His father opposed his wish to become an artist, and apprenticed him to a china dealer in London. From this he progressed to painting china at Turner's Manufactory at Brosely, Yorkshire, until about 1792 when he returned to London. After initial hardships, during which he determined to practice art at all costs, life broadened for him on his entering the Royal Academy schools and he subsequently joined the coterie of artists befriended by Dr. Monro. Cristall was a founder-member of the Society of Painters in Watercolours, formed in 1804; he was President of the Society in 1816 and 1819, and again from 1821 to 1831, but never prospered financially. He died in London on 18 October 1847, and was buried in Goodrich, Herefordshire, where he had lived for some years.

Cristall's early works in watercolor were large classical scenes, in the epic-pastoral manner then much admired. They have a certain heaviness, but are notable for their fine sense of composition and breadth of manner. Graham Reynolds sees Cristall as "the first to bring into water-colour that squareness and concentration on the basic facts of form" which may have contributed to the formation of Cotman's first and greatest style. In later years Cristall preferred to paint rustic and domestic figures in a robust manner which still has classical echoes. Of almost 500 watercolors which he exhibited at the Water-colour Society between 1805 and 1847, a large proportion are single figures of fisher folk, shepherds, or peasant girls spinning, bleaching linen, drawing water, or peeling vegetables. Martin Hardie's observation that "they are well-studied sturdy figures, with a natural rather than sentimental grandeur, poised, always firm on their feet" aptly describes the drawing exhibited here. Cristall's coloring is characteristic, favoring mauve-pink, clear yellowish-green and gray-blue, and a purplish chocolate brown.

85 A PEASANT GIRL SHADING HER EYES
Watercolor. 16¾ x 10¾ inches (42.6 x 27.5 cm.)

Inscribed: *J. C. 1812* lower left.

Provenance: L. G. Duke (D.943); Colnaghi 1960.

Literature: R. H. Wilenski, *An Outline of English Painting*, 1969, pl. 29a; Iolo Williams, *Early English Water-colours*, 1962, p. 347, pl. 219.

Exhibited: Royal Academy, *British Art*, 1934, no. 723, pl. CLXIII; 39 Grosvenor Square, London, *British Country Life*, 1937, no. 529; National Gallery, Washington, 1962, no. 25.

John Crome (1768–1821)

Crome was born in Norwich on 22 December 1768, the son of a journeyman weaver. His schooling was minimal: at twelve years of age he was employed as errand boy to a doctor. He committed himself as an apprentice for seven years to a coach and sign painter, during which time he developed a taste for painting landscape. With Robert Ladbrooke—later a celebrated painter, he shared a garret in which the two struggled to earn a living, Ladbrooke painting portraits, Crome landscapes. Thomas Harvey of Catton, a wealthy amateur and collector, was an invaluable friend to Crome. He instructed him in painting and gave him free access to study and make copies of English and Dutch paintings in his choice collection. Harvey's friend William Beechey, the portrait painter, also proved a great encourager of Crome's aspirations. In London, Crome acquired the experience that ensured his success as a painter on his return to Norwich. There he helped to inaugurate the Norwich Society of Artists in 1803, becoming its President in 1810. He exhibited thirteen paintings at the Royal Academy between 1806 and 1818.

As a teacher of drawing and painting, Crome was employed by various Norfolk families, forming a particularly affectionate friendship with that of the Quaker banker John Gurney, who had six daughters and a son, and sharing holiday excursions with them in many parts of England.

Crome was essentially a painter in oils. His watercolors are rare: the major examples are to be found mainly in the national collections. He was one of the few artists of that time to compose his own etchings, but, dissatisfied with his results, would not publish them. Thirteen years after his death, his widow published thirty-one of the etchings with the title *Norfolk Picturesque Scenery*.

In 1814 Crome went to France and Belgium, a visit which apparently satisfied his appetite for foreign travel; one painting, *Boulevard des Italiens*, was done in the following year but the *Fishmarket at Boulogne*, of similar continental flavor, was not painted until five years later. Crome died in Norwich on 22 April 1821.

86 A BOATLOAD

Watercolor. 4⅞ x 9⅛ inches (12.5 x 23.2 cm.)

Provenance: L. G. Duke (D.692); Colnaghi 1960.

Literature: Martin Hardie, II, pl. 49.

Exhibited: National Gallery, Washington, 1962, no. 27; V.M.F.A., Richmond, 1963, no. 166; Colnaghi, 1964–65, and Yale University Art Gallery, 1965, no. 70.

L.G. Duke notes that "the drawing closely resembles in feeling Crome's painting of *A Barge with a Wounded Soldier, circa* 1815, illustrated in C. H. Collins Baker, *Crome*, 1921, pl. XXIII." The painting is now in the Mellon collection.

Robert Hills (1769–1844)

Hills was born in Islington, London, on 26 June 1769. He had some early lessons from the drawing-master John Alexander Gresse, and in 1788 entered the Royal Academy schools. Hills made his name as a painter of animals—sheep, cattle, and particularly deer. He carefully studied both the anatomy and the habits of the different species, and would stalk a stag all day to secure a sketch, following it into the recesses of the forest "like a sportsman sighting his game." Between 1798 and 1815 he published a fine series of 780 etchings of animals, modestly offered as "groups for the embellishment of landscape." Hills was often invited by other artists, such as Barrett, Robson, and Nesfield, to enliven their landscapes with groups of cattle or deer. Though his own pictures are mainly of animals, many have specific landscape backgrounds in Windsor Park, the Lake District, Surrey, or Kent; and occasionally, in his delicate drawings of cottages and farmyards, the animals graze altogether out of the picture. Hills made one excursion abroad, in 1815, a month after Waterloo; he traversed the battlefield and made a series of sketches, some of which were published in his *Sketches in Flanders and Belgium*. Hills was an amiable and respected figure, with many friends among artists. He was a founder-member in 1804 of the Society of Painters in Water-colours, and its first secretary; he exhibited nearly 600 works there between 1805 and 1844. He died in London on 14 May 1844.

Hills's early work is in quiet, silvery tones, with flat washes over pencil or pen-and-ink outline. In time his sureness of touch and sense of spontaneity deserted him, leaving, in Basil Long's words, "prettiness without power." His best work was done about 1810–20. By then he had developed a characteristic stippling touch, by which he could skillfully suggest the texture of an animal's fur, the bark of an old tree, the straw in a farmyard, or the snow in a winter landscape; and his pastoral scenes of this period charm the eye not because he idealizes but because he understands in detail the daily round of rural life.

87 A VILLAGE SNOW SCENE, 1819

Watercolor. 12¾ x 16¾ inches (32.4 x 42.5 cm.)

Inscribed: R. Hills *1819* lower right corner.

Provenance: T. Girtin; Tom Girtin; John Baskett 1970.

Literature: Laurence Binyon, *English Water-colours*, 1933, p. 93; Martin Hardie, II, p. 140, pl. 115.

Exhibited: Tokyo, Institute of Art Research, 1929, pl. XLII; Graves Art Gallery, Sheffield, *Early Water-colours from the Collection of Thomas Girtin Jnr.*, 1953, no. 62; Leeds City Art Gallery, *Early English Water-colours*, 1958, no. 65; Royal Academy, *The Girtin Collection*, 1962, no. 59.

Henry Edridge, A.R.A. (1769–1821)

Edridge was born in Paddington in August 1769, the son of a London tradesman. He was apprenticed to the artist and engraver William Pether, and later entered the Royal Academy schools, where, with the encouragement of Sir Joshua Reynolds, his talent for portraiture developed. Beginning as a miniaturist, he later evolved an individual style of portrait-drawing, largely in monochrome, touching faces and hands with watercolor while the remainder is an intricate combination of pencil, pen, and wash. A series of portraits of his fellow-artists (in the Print Room of the British Museum) includes a slight but debonair study of Girtin sketching, and an admirable portrait of Edridge's lifelong friend Thomas Hearne.

Portraiture continued to be the mainstay of Edridge's professional career, and to account for most of his 260 Royal Academy exhibits. With Hearne's encouragement, he began to make landscape drawings. This side of his work, undertaken primarily for his own pleasure, is less well known; but his cottages and farm scenes, rural lanes and wooded villages have the same intimate, delicate quality as his portraits. Edridge was a member of the Monro circle, but as friend rather than protégé of Dr. Monro. Farington describes a sketching excursion in Surrey in 1803, with "Dr. Monro and Edridge in one gig, and Hoppner and I in another." Edridge first exhibited landscapes at the Royal Academy in 1814. In 1817 and 1819 he made sketching excursions to France, and began to exhibit views of architecture in Normandy and Paris: their technique and fine detail influenced the later though more heavy-handed work of Samuel Prout. Edridge died in London on 23 April 1821, and was buried beside Hearne in Bushey churchyard.

88 STREAM WITH TREES AND CATTLE

Watercolor. 16 x 10¾ inches (40.8 x 27.5 cm.)

Inscribed: *Bromley Hill, Oct* *11, 1807* in pencil lower left, repeated on verso.

Provenance: Sabina Girtin; Tom Girtin; John Baskett 1970.

Exhibited: Graves Art Gallery, Sheffield, *Early Water-colours from the Collection of Thomas Girtin Jnr.*, 1953, no. 29.

James Ward, R.A. (1769–1859)

Ward was born in London on 23 October 1769. His whole life, from his tough boyhood in Thames Street, where his alcoholic father managed a wholesale fruit business, to his declining years, short of money and surrounded by difficult and frequently bickering relatives, appears as one long struggle against adversity.

Ward worked for three years of his childhood as a bottle-washer in a London warehouse, before being apprenticed at the age of twelve to the eminent engraver John Raphael Smith. This arrangement lasted only a few months; James's elder brother William, who had completed his own apprenticeship to Smith, took the boy away with him to Kensal Green, then a village outside London. James served an apprenticeship of eight years with his brother from 1783 to 1791, living in his house part of the time. In 1786 James's sister Ann married the painter George Morland and a month later William married Morland's sister Maria.

James Ward developed a rare skill as an engraver, and in 1794 was appointed Painter and Engraver in Mezzotinto to the Prince of Wales. (Later in life he presented proof impressions of all his mezzotints, totaling 400, to the British Museum.) However, against the advice of his friends and patrons and despite initial loss of earnings, Ward devoted more and more of his time to painting rather than engraving. His early paintings and drawings were modeled closely on those of his brother-in-law Morland, both in subject matter and technique. But a later and more significant influence on his style came from studying the works of Rubens. It is well known that Ward's first large-scale animal painting, *Bulls Fighting, with a view of St. Donat's Castle in the background*, was painted in direct emulation of Rubens' *Château de Steen*, then owned by Sir George Beaumont. It is clear from Ward's output that he must also have seen and studied other Rubens paintings and drawings, and he retained a lifelong admiration for the great Flemish artist. Another considerable influence on Ward, as regards his drawings, came from Thomas Girtin. Ward made a free copy of Girtin's *Cayne Falls*, now in the British Museum (L.B. IV, no. 32), and many of his early landscape drawings reveal a Girtinesque feeling for color and composition.

Ward's personality was such that he always responded energetically to a challenge, and we owe his masterpiece, the immense painting of *Gordale Scar, Yorkshire*, to the fact that Ward had been told that it was an impossible subject to paint. The painting, for which there are many preliminary studies, was completed in 1814, and is one of the key works of British romantic art.

Ward, who was elected an Associate of the Royal Academy in 1807 and a full member four years later, was enormously industrious. He exhibited ninety pictures at the British Institution between 1806 and 1846, and 298 at the Royal Academy between 1792 and 1855, the eighty-seventh year of his life. Ward's ability to portray animals brought him a number of influential patrons, with some of whom he remained on close terms for the rest of his life. But financial success did not last. In 1815 the directors of the British Institution presented Ward with a prize of 1,000 guineas for his allegorical sketch *The Triumph of the Duke of Wellington*, and commissioned him to paint a finished work for the Royal Hospital, Chelsea. The results for Ward were disastrous, and marked a turning point in his career. His over-ambitious design took six years to complete, involved him in great expense, and when finished was severely criticized. Disenchanted, he retired from London to spend the last thirty years of his life at Roundcroft Cottage, Cheshunt, largely isolated from the life of the Academy, his patrons, and fellow-artists. He died there on 16 November 1859, aged ninety.

James Ward was a prolific draughtsman with a vigorous technique which he applied to a wide range of subjects—landscapes, portraits, figure drawings, *genre*, religious subjects, and especially birds and animals. The great majority of his drawings were made before his retirement to the country—later drawings are rare—but he took great pride in showing visitors his portfolio of studies, which he mounted himself in a characteristic style, and almost all of which he signed with his initials and the letters "R.A.".

89 STUDIES OF GEESE

Watercolor touched with gum. 11 x 18 inches (28 x 45.5 cm.)

Inscribed: *JWD . R.A.* lower left and *No. 1* top left in pencil. (Repaired lower right corner.)

Provenance: Martin Hardie; Colnaghi 1961.

Exhibited: V.M.F.A., Richmond, 1963, no. 463.

William Daniell, R.A. (1769–1837)

Daniell, born at Chertsey, Surrey, was the nephew of Thomas Daniell who took him to India at the age of fifteen. He was described as "assistant engraver" to avoid an official restriction imposed on the flow of artists to that country. The journey out took a circuitous route via China, and the drawings made there were used later on for book illustrations, and paintings of the tea trade. On return to England in 1794, uncle and nephew collaborated in the magnificent publication *Oriental Scenery*, in six series, each of twenty-four folio-size aquatints, and taking thirteen years to complete. Their industry was prodigious; they even found time during this great work to make numerous large plates and illustrations for other books. Between 1795 and his death, William exhibited over 160 paintings at the Royal Academy and sixty-one at the British Institution. At thirty he became a "student" at the Academy schools, an Associate in 1807, and full Academician in 1822.

Another extensive and attractive work, *The Voyage Round Great Britain*, took twelve years to complete. The ambitious tour, planned to record views with a camera obscura by Daniell and a descriptive text by a friend, Richard Ayton, was ultimately recorded in eight volumes, with over 300 aquatints. Ayton, an erratic young man with a gift for mercurial words, withdrew after writing for the first two volumes, Daniell providing a rather leaden text for the rest. Few complete sets exist as the plates are demanded singly for their attractive topography. Following this publication Daniell concentrated on Windsor and its environs, making watercolors and aquatints, and his oil painting of *The Long Walk* is considered his masterpiece. Yet another of Daniell's successes was a large series of portraits of notable people done in soft-ground etching from drawings by George Dance.

Daniell's work stands secure on the high level set by the very talented artists of his generation, and its standard was maintained up to the last. He died, after much suffering, on 16 August 1837.

90 WINDSOR CASTLE FROM NEAR THE BROCAS MEADOWS, 1827

Watercolor. 12 x 19¾ inches (30.5 x 50.1 cm.)

Inscribed: *W. Daniell / 1827* lower left.

Provenance: Agnew 1961.

Engraved: Same size in aquatint, by Daniell himself.

François Louis Thomas Francia (1772–1839)

Louis Francia, generally so-called, was born in Calais on 21 December 1772. His father, a refugee, brought him when young to England. He was employed as an assistant in a drawing school run by Joseph Charles Barrow, where he was described by J. P. Neale, topographic draughtsman, as "a conceited French refugee, who used to amuse the party with his blundering absurdities." Even so, he remained in this post for thirteen years, having a high regard for Barrow's talents and personal charm. Barrow was also John Varley's drawing-master. Francia struck up a friendship with Girtin, having met the latter at Dr. Monro's house in the Adelphi, and became secretary to a group of artists known as "The Brothers," who met to compose "Historic landscape" with subjects chosen from "poetick passages."

Francia exhibited eighty-five items at the Royal Academy from 1795 to 1821, but was unsuccessful in an election for an Associate there in 1816. He was also painter in watercolors to the Duchess of York. His work up to about 1810 bore a strong similarity to that of Girtin, each influencing the work of the other. After 1810 a more romantic trend infiltrated his compositions, and the mood of his landscapes and seascapes altered key; Martin Hardie considers that he "deserves credit as one of the first to discover that there could be beauty in sombre landscape." At this time he made and published some forty soft-ground etchings "imitated from originals" of Gainsborough, Hoppner, Girtin, S. and W. Owen, Callcott, and John Varley. In 1817 he was back in his native Calais, his mind full of all that was best in English drawing. Bonington, then fifteen, was seen sketching on the quayside by Francia, who gave him free lessons in drawing, and expounded, with the help of the "imitated" originals, on the lines Bonington should follow. In so doing, there later resulted Bonington's own brilliant interpretations in watercolor, which in turn were to influence other artists in France and especially Francia's own later drawings. Thus Francia's role of catalyst was perhaps his most valuable contribution. He outlived his pupil's short life by ten years, dying in Calais on 6 February 1839.

91 MOUSEHOLD HEATH, NORWICH

Watercolor. 12⅜ x 9⅛ inches (31.5 x 23 cm.)

Inscribed: *L. Francia* and, verso, *Done for his friend Wm. Peirson* [sic] *as a small return for his Imitations of Kobell's Etchings by L. Francia 1808.*

Provenance: L. G. Duke (D.496); Colnaghi 1961.

Literature: Martin Hardie, ɪɪ, pl. 125.

Exhibited: Eton College, *Loan Exhibition of English Drawings from the Collection of L. G. Duke*, 1948, no. 26; Arts Council, *Three Centuries of British Water-colours and Drawings*, 1951, no. 66; National Gallery, Washington, 1962, no. 32; V.M.F.A., Richmond, 1963, no. 168; Colnaghi, 1964–65, and Yale University Art Gallery, 1965, no. 44.

George Chinnery, R.H.A. (1774–1852)

Chinnery was born in London in 1774. His father, an East India merchant, was an amateur artist. No information about Chinnery's artistic training exists, but in 1791, at the age of seventeen, he began to exhibit portraits at the Royal Academy. In 1797 he established himself as a portrait painter in Dublin, and married there; but in 1802 he deserted his wife and children and sailed for India, where he lived for the next twenty years or so, painting portraits and also making pen and watercolor studies of landscapes and figures. Sir Charles D'Oyly, Collector of the district of Dacca and a gifted amateur artist, considered Chinnery "the ablest limner in the land"; he was Chinnery's pupil as well as his admirer, himself drew in Chinnery's manner, and lithographed many of Chinnery's designs. Chinnery's character was, as William Hickey put it, "extremely odd and eccentric—so much so as at times to make me think him deranged." His inability to manage his own finances was notorious. The unwanted arrival of his wife in India in 1818 further embarrassed him, and in 1825, leaving her and £40,000 of debts behind, he decamped to China, where he lived first at Canton and then at Macao until his death, in straitened circumstances, on 30 May 1852.

Chinnery painted in a great variety of media: oil, pastel, gouache, and watercolors. His portrait drawings, done in pencil with faces tinted in watercolor, are much in the manner of Cosway. His pen drawings of figures and landscapes are as swift and cursive as the shorthand notes he habitually made on them; and his topography was remarkably accurate. In both oil and watercolor his coloring was direct, with reds and blues emphasized in a manner that is individual and recognizable.

92 FIGURE SEATED BY AN INDIAN TEMPLE
Gouache. 9⅝ x 11¼ inches (24.5 x 28.4 cm.)
Provenance: Ralph Edwards, C.B.E.; John Baskett 1969.

Thomas Girtin (1775–1802)

Girtin was born in London on 18 February 1775, the son of a brushmaker. His drawing-master was a Mr. Fisher, about whom nothing is known. Girtin was apprenticed to Edward Dayes on 15 May 1789; but a few known facts point to there being little sympathy between their natures. Turner came into Girtin's life about this time, when both were said to have been employed coloring prints for John Raphael Smith. Dayes's influence on both was strong: his handling of watercolor in the traditional style and method was emulated by them so closely that drawings by any of the three done between 1792 and 1794 are very difficult to attribute correctly without due evidence.

Girtin's association with Dayes lasted until almost 1795. They collaborated in copying drawings done by James Moore, linen draper and antiquary, for his publications of antiquarian remains. Over the years 1794 to 1797, Girtin and Turner spent many evenings together at Dr. Monro's hospitable house, copying drawings by early English artists, notably

J. R. Cozens. In 1794 Girtin started the first of his extensive sketching tours, traveling with James Moore in the Midlands and drawing castles and cathedrals. *Ely Cathedral*, Girtin's first exhibit at the Royal Academy, was based on a drawing by Moore. It is from this time forward that the real creative bud in Girtin broke into blossom, owing no doubt to the freedom he found in no longer drawing from the works of others for his living. His method, too, changed from the accepted practice of laying a foundation of gray undertone before applying watercolor, to using warmer and related colors as a basis, as in oil painting. His distinguished patrons included the Earl of Elgin, the Earl of Essex, Lord Mulgrave, Sir George Beaumont, Lady Long (afterwards Lady Farnborough), and Lord Harewood and his son Edward Lascelles, who kept a room at Harewood especially for Girtin's visits from 1798 to 1801. Girtin was one of the founder-members of a sketching society bearing the homely title, "The Brothers," which attracted some important artists to fraternal gatherings in a room once used by Reynolds for painting, and later occupied by Dr. Johnson.

Large panoramas were popular at this time, and Girtin planned a giant circular view of London, calling it the *Eidometropolis*. Five drawings for this enterprise are in the British Museum. The work was accomplished and exhibited in 1802. It is not known whether the medium was oil or tempera; it was sold in 1825, taken to Russia, and has not been heard of since. Girtin had ideas for a similar project of Paris, but while there in 1801, signs of rapidly approaching ill-health became evident. Even so, he drew and etched twenty views of Paris and its environs, published posthumously by his brother John in 1803.

A brilliant and industrious artist, Girtin, had he lived, would have complemented Turner as a supreme pillar of the British school in both quality and output, although from the indications Girtin left, his oeuvre would have been totally different in character from Turner's. He died in London on 9 November 1802; legend has it that the Lord Mayor's procession was about to pass the house in the Strand as he died. He was buried in St. Paul's, Covent Garden.

93 THE OUSE BRIDGE, YORK, 1800

Watercolor. 12⅞ x 20⅝ inches (32.7 x 52.4 cm.)

Inscribed: *Girtin 1800* lower center.

Provenance: T. C. Girtin; G. W. Girtin; T. Girtin; Tom Girtin; John Baskett 1970.

Literature: N. Lytton, *Water-colour*, 1911, pl. 9; Randall Davies, *Thomas Girtin's Watercolours*, *The Studio*, 1924, pl. 78; T. Girtin and D. Loshak, *The Art of Thomas Girtin*, 1954, no. 382(i), fig. 63.

Engraved: In mezzotint by S. W. Reynolds, *Liber Naturae*, 1 May 1824, reprinted 1883.

Exhibited: Burlington Fine Arts Club, *British Water-colour Artists born before 1800*, 1871, no. 100, and *Thomas Girtin*, 1875, no. 119; Grosvenor Gallery, *Water-colour Drawings by deceased Masters of the British School*, 1911, no. 185; Tate Gallery, 1920; Royal Academy, *The First Hundred Years of the Royal Academy 1769–1868*, 1951–52, no. 511; Agnew, *Loan Exhibition of Water-colour Drawings by Girtin*, 1953, no. 30; Graves Art Gallery, Sheffield, *Early Water-colours from the Collection of Thomas Girtin Jnr.*, 1953, no. 51; Leeds City Art Gallery, *Early English Water-colours*, 1958, no. 49; Royal Academy, *The Girtin Collection*, 1962, no. 161.

94 THE NEW WALK, YORK

Watercolor. 12¼ x 21¾ inches (31.1 x 55.8 cm.)

Inscribed: *Girtin* lower left.

Provenance: Tiffen, 1860; G. W. Girtin; T. Girtin; Tom Girtin; John Baskett 1970.

Literature: C. R. Grundy, "The Loan Collection of Drawings by Girtin at the Fitzwilliam Museum," *Connoisseur*, June 1921, ill. p. 86; T. Girtin and D. Loshak, *The Art of Thomas Girtin*, 1954, no. 247(i).

Exhibited: Burlington Fine Arts Club, *Thomas Girtin*, 1875, no. 89; Fitzwilliam Museum, Cambridge, *Loan Collection of Drawings by Girtin*, 1920, no. 22; Leeds City Art Gallery, *Sixty Pictures of Yorkshire Scenery*, 1937, no. 25; Louvre, Paris, *La Peinture Anglaise XVIIIe & XIXe Siècles*, 1938, no. 207; Agnew, *Loan Exhibition of Water-colour Drawings by Girtin*, 1953, no. 94; Graves Art Gallery, Sheffield, *Early Water-colours from the Collection of Thomas Girtin Jnr.*, 1953, no. 47; Royal Academy, *The Girtin Collection*, 1962, no. 142; Victoria, 1971, no. 17.

95 LYME REGIS

Watercolor. 8¾ x 17⅛ inches (22.2 x 43.4 cm.)

Provenance: Spink 1967.

This drawing was probably done in the summer of 1797 when Girtin toured the south-western counties. Several drawings from this tour were exhibited at the Royal Academy in the following spring.

96 THE ABBEY MILL, KNARESBOROUGH

Watercolor. 12⅝ x 20⅝ inches (32.2 x 52.3 cm.)

Inscribed: Verso *Mr. Reynolds Poland St. Soho No. 46* (?), in pencil.

Provenance: E. K. Greg; J. C. Butterwick; Sir George Davies; Lady Davies to her daughter, Mrs. Streatfield; Agnew; Sir William Worsley; Agnew 1971.

Literature: T. Girtin and D. Loshak, *The Art of Thomas Girtin*, 1954, no. 437(ii).

Exhibited: Leeds City Art Gallery, *Early English Water-colours*, 1958, no. 53; Agnew, *Loan Exhibition of Water-colour Drawings by Thomas Girtin*, 1953, no. 94.

There is a pencil sketch of this view in the Girtin sketchbook, published by Martin Hardie (Walpole Society, vol. xxvii, 1938–39, p. 93, no. 8, pl. xivb), who notes "The drawing is inscribed *At Knaresborough*, and the exact locality was identified by Lord Harewood, who writes 'There is still a tiny island where Girtin has put in a little tuft of vegetation below the mill wheel, but it has quite a respectable tree on it now.' "

Joseph Mallord William Turner, R.A. (1775–1851)

Turner was born in Maiden Lane, Covent Garden, London on 23 April 1775, the son of a barber. Although highly intelligent, his formal education was scanty and in later life this was reflected in the difficulty he found in expressing himself lucidly either on paper or when speaking in public. At the age of fourteen, Turner entered the Royal Academy schools and exhibited his first watercolor at the Royal Academy in 1790. For the next sixty years hardly a summer exhibition passed without Turner being represented; he was one of the Academy's most devoted supporters, serving on many of its committees and greatly enjoying the companionship of his fellow-artists there. About 1794, he and Girtin began to visit Dr. Monro's house and were there introduced to—and made to copy—the watercolors of John Robert Cozens and other eighteenth-century topographical draughtsmen: work in a tradition which Turner was first to build on and then to transform.

Turner was a prodigious traveler; as a young man he toured part of the British Isles each summer collecting material for the next year's exhibition, stumping along on his short legs "twenty to twenty-five miles a day, with his little modicum of baggage at the end of a stick." Later, he also traveled extensively on the Continent, especially in France, Switzerland, and Italy, covering page after page of his sketchbooks with rapid pencil drawings, sometimes coloring these in the evening in his inn room but more usually relying on his phenomenal visual memory to transform—sometimes many years later—what often amounted to no more than a few lines into finished watercolors or oils. For instance, when invited by Sir Walter Scott to visit Abbotsford in 1831 to make drawings to illustrate a complete edition of Scott's *Poems*, Turner tried to get out of going by saying that he already had drawings in his sketchbooks from much earlier tours for most of the subjects proposed.

By about 1830 Turner's technical mastery, coupled with his daring sense of color, enabled him to achieve effects in watercolor which were truly revolutionary. His late drawings and oils were much criticized in spite of Ruskin's championship in *Modern Painters*, but Turner never lacked patrons. They and Turner's work for the engravers (almost 800 prints after his work were published in his lifetime) earned him a large fortune. This by no means altered his style of living: his dress remained careless if not slovenly, and the roof leaked in his unheated studio. He became more and more of a recluse; finally his "digestion failed thro' loss of teeth" and he died at his cottage by the Thames, 119 Cheyne Row, Chelsea, on 19 December 1851. Turner's will was muddled and much contested but the most important result was that the contents of his studio became the property of the nation. This comprised about 300 oil paintings which are now in the Tate Gallery and over 19,000 watercolors and pencil sketches now in the British Museum, the output of a long life of continuous work (Turner's only recreation was fishing). The twelve watercolors exhibited here illustrate something of the extraordinary variety of Turner's work in watercolor, showing a range and development unrivaled by any other British artist.

97 NEWARK-UPON-TRENT

Watercolor. 11 15/16 x 16 9/16 inches (30.3 x 42.1 cm.)
Inscribed: Verso *J.M.W. Turner Newark-upon-Trent* in pencil.
Provenance: P. R. Bennett 1971.

In the summer of 1794 Turner made a tour of the Midlands to collect material for drawings to be engraved, a number of which were published in the *Copper Plate Magazine* at intervals in the next three years. Turner's plans for the trip can be found at the beginning of the *Matlock* sketchbook of 1794 in the Turner Bequest in the British Museum: on page 4 he has noted, "Newark, a Bridge, and Gothic Church and Castle." There is also a pencil drawing, 8 x 10¾ inches, of Newark Castle, of about the same date, on a loose sheet of paper in the British Museum.

This watercolor must date from about 1795, and shows Turner working in the traditional eighteenth-century topographical manner. The elongated figures, typical of Turner's work at this period, show the influence of Edward Dayes.

98 THE MER DE GLACE AND SOURCE OF THE ARVEYRON, CHAMONIX

Watercolor. 27 x 40 inches (68.5 x 101.5 cm.)
Provenance: Walter Fawkes of Farnley and descendants, from its acquisition *circa* 1803 to 1961; Agnew 1961.
Literature: F. Wedmore, *Turner and Ruskin*, 1900, opposite p. 100; Sir Walter Armstrong, *Turner*, 1902, p. 246; Charles Holmes, *The Genius of J.M.W. Turner, The Studio*, 1903, pl. 47; A. J. Finberg, *Turner's Water-colours at Farnley Hall*, 1915, p. 21, no. 9; A. J. Finberg, *The Life of J. M. W. Turner R.A.*, 1961, pp. 101, 466, 481, 503; Martin Hardie, II, pl. 18.
Exhibited: Royal Academy, 1803, no. 396 (as *Glacier, and source of the Arveron, going up to the Mer de Glace, in the valley of Chumouni*); Grosvenor Place (Walter Fawkes's London house), 1819, no. 39; Leeds, 1839, no. 61; Leeds City Art Gallery, *Turner Watercolours from Farnley Hall*, 1948, no. 4; Agnew, *Centenary Loan Exhibition of Turner Watercolours*, 1951, no. 45; The Holburne of Menstruie Museum of Art, Bath, *Turner Watercolours from Farnley Hall*, 1959, no. 1; Gerson Gallery, New York, *Turner Water-colours*, 1960, no. 9; V.M.F.A., Richmond, 1963, no. 146; Agnew, *Turner*, 1967, no. 41.

During the Peace of Amiens in 1802 Turner seized the opportunity to visit the Continent for the first time. After studying the works of art exhibited in the Louvre which Napoleon had plundered from Italy, Turner set out for Switzerland and the Alps, the real goal of his journey. There, although he told Farington that he found the wine too acid and underwent much fatigue from walking, he considered that the country "on the whole surpasses Wales, and Scotland too," and he saw "very fine Thunderstorms among the Mountains." The Alpine scenery provided him with subjects after his own heart and he responded with a series of watercolors rightly described by Ruskin as "quite stupendous." The engraving in the *Liber Studiorum* of *The Source of the Arveron*, published in 1816, differs considerably from this watercolor.

99 WEYMOUTH

Watercolor. 5½ x 8⅜ inches (14 x 21.3 cm.)

Inscribed: *J.M.W. Turner R.A.* lower right.

Provenance: B. G. Windus; C. S. Bale, sold Christie's 14 May 1881, lot 196, bought McLean; W. Sturdy; A. T. Hollingsworth; E. Bulmer; Agnew 1961.

Literature: Sir Walter Armstrong, *Turner*, 1902, p. 284; W. G. Rawlinson, *The Engraved Work of J. M. W. Turner R.A.*, vol. I, 1908, p. 49, no. 91; vol. II, 1913, no. 190; A. J. Finberg, *Life of J. M. W. Turner R.A.*, 1961, pp. 182, 483, no. 269.

Engraved: By W. B. Cooke for *Picturesque Views of the Southern Coast of England*, 1814.

Exhibited: Cooke's Gallery, 9 Soho Square, 1822, no. 111; Leggatt Bros., *Turner*, 1960, no. 14; National Gallery, Washington, 1962, no. 88 (ill.); Colnaghi, 1964–65, and Yale University Art Gallery, 1965, no. 34.

Drawn *circa* 1811–12. Turner visited Weymouth about the end of July 1811, in a two-month tour of the West Country collecting material to be engraved for Cooke's *Southern Coast*, during which he traveled well over 600 miles and made more than 200 pencil sketches.

This watercolor is an unusually fine example of this series which shows the skill Turner had acquired in depicting views of vast expanse on a very small scale.

Portland Bill can be seen in the distance.

100 DARTMOOR: THE SOURCE OF THE TAMAR AND THE TORRIDGE

Watercolor. 8 x 12⅝ inches (20.3 x 32 cm.)

Provenance: J. Gillott, sold Christie's 4 May 1872, lot 105, bought Agnew; J. Heugh, sold Christie's 24 April 1874, lot 85, bought Agnew; H. Gaskell, sold Christie's 24 June 1909, bought Agnew; H. M. Robinson; R. Brocklebank; W. West; G. H. and R. H. Gaskell; Mrs. E. Walton-Brown; J. M. A. Day; Agnew 1962.

Exhibited: Royal Academy, 1886, no. 28; Wolverhampton, *The Gaskell Collection of Landscape Paintings by English Masters*, 1955; V.M.F.A., Richmond, 1963, no. 147.

Drawn *circa* 1813, when Turner paid a second visit to Devon (see no. 99), making his headquarters at Plymouth. He seems to have explored the southwest part of the county pretty thoroughly and over 400 pencil sketches survive as a record of his stay.

Although engraved by W. B. Cooke for *The Rivers of Devon*, this work (advertised by Cooke about 1818) never actually appeared under this title. Probably the failure of the *Views in Sussex*, issued 1816–20, led to its being abandoned, and the four plates which had been engraved were later sold separately. The print of *The Source of the Tamar and the Torridge* remained unfinished until about 1850.

101 ON THE WASHBURN

Watercolor. 10¾ x 15⅜ inches (27.2 x 40 cm.)

Inscribed: *J. M. W. Turner R.A.* lower left.

Provenance: Abel Buckley; C. Fairfax Murray; Sir William Mills; N. H. Rollason; Agnew 1963.

Literature: A. J. Finberg, *Life of J. M. W. Turner R.A.*, 1961, p. 228.

Exhibited: Royal Academy, *Old Masters*, 1908, no. 217; Agnew, *Turner, Cox and De Wint*, 1924, no. 116; Colnaghi, 1964–65, and Yale University Art Gallery, 1965, no. 35.

This drawing was formerly known as *On the Wharfe*, but really depicts the Washburn. The two rivers meet not far from Farnley Hall, near Otley in Yorkshire, the home of Walter Ramsden Fawkes who was Turner's close friend and biggest patron during the first half of his career. When Fawkes died in 1825, his collection of Turners at Farnley Hall comprised seven oil paintings and over 200 watercolors (see also no. 98). Turner seems to have felt more at home at Farnley than anywhere else, even Petworth, although he could never bring himself to go there again after Walter Fawkes's death.

Turner was at Farnley early in August 1815 and probably painted this watercolor then. Fawkes may have ordered it after seeing an unfinished study (11 x 17½ inches; sold Christie's 9 November 1971, lot 120, and now also in the Mellon collection), a page from a sketchbook which may possibly date from a slightly earlier visit.

A rather similar watercolor, entitled *A Lonely Dale, Wharfedale*, also with a kingfisher in it, is in the City Art Gallery, Leeds.

102 LEEDS, 1816

Watercolor. 11½ x 16¾ inches (29 x 42.5 cm.)

Inscribed: *J. M. W. Turner R.A. 1816* in ink lower left.

Provenance: John Allnutt, sold Christie's 1863, bought Vokins; John Knowles of Manchester, sold Christie's 5 June 1880, lot 484, bought Fine Art Society; sold Christie's 22 July 1882, lot 65, bought McLean; Mrs. Lee; A. G. Turner, to his son J. G. Turner; Agnew 1962.

Literature: Sir Walter Armstrong, *Turner*, 1902, p. 261; W. G. Rawlinson, *The Engraved Work of J. M. W. Turner R.A.*, vol. II, 1913, pp. 214, 407.

Engraved: By J. D. Harding, 1823, for a later edition of Whitaker's *Loidis and Elmete* (a history of Leeds) originally published 1816–20.

Exhibited: Manchester, *Art Treasures Exhibition*, 1857, no. 312; Colnaghi, 1964–65, and Yale University Art Gallery, 1965, no. 37.

Three pencil sketches connected with this watercolor are in the British Museum, in the *Devonshire Rivers* no. 3 and *Wharfedale* sketchbook of 1812–15, Inventory no. CXXXIV, pages 37a, 38, 79, and 80. Pages 79 and 80 show a general panorama of the city while the other two drawings are confined to details. These sketches were most probably made in the summer of 1815 when Turner was staying at Farnley Hall (see no. 101), which is only eleven miles from Leeds.

The watercolor was probably painted to be engraved in Dr. Whitaker's *Loidis and Elmete*. This was the title of the second volume of his *History and Topography of the Town and Parish of Leeds and Parts Adjacent*, published in 1816. A later edition of 1823 is said to include this plate, engraved by J. D. Harding.

Armstrong and Rawlinson both err in stating that this drawing once belonged to Ruskin.

103 VESUVIUS IN ERUPTION, 1817

Watercolor. 11 x 15½ inches (28 x 38.5 cm.)

Inscribed: Verso *Mount Vesuvius in Eruption / J M W Turner R A 1817* in pencil.

Provenance: Walter Fawkes of Farnley (where it remained until 1890); W. Newall, 1922; Sir Robert Hadfield; Brian Hamilton, sold Sotheby's 22 November 1961, lot 48; Colnaghi 1962.

Literature: W. Thornbury, *Life and Correspondence of Turner*, 1877, pp. 176, 633; Sir Walter Armstrong, *Turner*, 1902, p. 283; W. G. Rawlinson, *The Engraved Work of J. M. W. Turner R.A.*, vol. II, 1913, pp. 197, 228; A. J. Finberg, *Turner's Water-colours at Farnley Hall*, 1915, p. 28, no. 196; A. J. Finberg, *The Life of J. M. W. Turner R.A.*, 1961, p. 273 and nos. 256, 521.

Engraved: By W. B. Cooke as the frontispiece to *Delineations of Pompeii* (date uncertain); and by T. Jeavons for *Friendship's Offering*, 1830.

Exhibited: Cooke's Gallery, 1822, no. 8; Leeds, 1839, no. 80; Loan Exhibition, Guildhall, 1899, no. 145.

The volcano is seen by night across the Bay of Naples from the shore near Posilippo, with the Castel dell'Ovo in the middle distance.

It is difficult to believe that this does not record a scene which Turner had witnessed, especially as we know that when he was in Rome in October 1819, Vesuvius began to erupt, and Turner hurried down to Naples to observe it. Yet the date of 1817 on the reverse seems to be correct, which means that Turner must have made this drawing before he first visited Italy, basing it on a print or drawing by another artist. There is evidence both in Turner's sketchbooks in the British Museum and from W. B. Cooke's account books that Turner had two drawings of *Vesuvius* in hand for Cooke *circa* 1817 and that he received thirty guineas for the pair in 1818.

When Cooke's exhibition of watercolors was opened at his gallery at no. 9 Soho Square in 1822, Robert Hunt in the *Spectator* for 3 February described this drawing as "a reddened, yellowed and delicious horror."

104 THE UPPER FALLS OF THE REICHENBACH

Watercolor. 11 x 15½ inches (27.8 x 39.4 cm.)

Provenance: Walter Fawkes and descendants until 1937; acquired by S. Girtin and T. Girtin from Agnew 1938; Tom Girtin; John Baskett 1970.

Literature: Sir Walter Armstrong, *Turner*, 1902, p. 272; A. J. Finberg, *Turner's Water-colours at Farnley Hall*, 1915, p. 28, pl. XVI; A. J. Finberg, *Life of J. M. W. Turner R.A.*, 1961, nos. 245, 498.

Exhibited: Grosvenor Place (Walter Fawkes's London house), 1819, no. 36; Leeds, 1839, no. 23 or 29; Royal Academy, Winter Exhibition, 1886, no. 33; Grafton Gallery, *Old Masters*, 1911, no. 212; Agnew, 1938, no. 144; Graves Art Gallery, Sheffield, *Early Water-colours from the Collection of Thomas Girtin Jnr.*, 1953, no. 102; Norwich Castle Museum, *English Water-colours c. 1750–c. 1820*, 1955, no. 46; Leeds City Art Gallery, *Early English Water-colours*, 1958, no. 116; Royal Academy, *The Girtin Collection*, 1962, no. 81.

Drawn *circa* 1818 (in dating it *circa* 1804 Armstrong has confused it with a large upright drawing of the Falls which also belonged to Walter Fawkes), but based on much earlier sketches made during Turner's visit to Switzerland in 1802. A related study, a page out of the *St. Gothard* sketchbook, is in the collection of Lady Courtauld.

Finberg points out that the white dress of the girl and the white dog lower left have been dug out by Turner with a penknife.

105 PATTERDALE

Watercolor. 11 x 15⅝ inches (28 x 39.5 cm.). Watermark *J. Whatman, Turkey Mill*.
Inscribed: *J. M. W. Turner RA* lower left.
Provenance: J. Gillott 1872; Albert Levy; John Heugh 1878; Sir William Agnew, Bart. 1910; C. Morland Agnew 1931; Hugh L. Agnew; Agnew 1965.
Literature: Sir Walter Armstrong, *Turner*, 1902, p. 270; A. J. Finberg, *Early English Water-colour Drawings*, The Studio, 1919, p. 9, no. 21, pl. VIII; Martin Hardie, II, pl. 19.
Exhibited: Royal Academy, 1886, no. 27.

Drawn *circa* 1820. Patterdale is in the Lake District, near Ullswater. The church in the foreground was pulled down and a new one built soon afterwards. An earlier drawing of Patterdale was engraved in Mawman's *Excursion to the Highlands of Scotland in 1805*. The only pencil drawings of Patterdale are in the *Tweed and Lakes* sketchbook which Turner used on his extensive northern tour in the summer of 1797.

106 FOLKESTONE

Watercolor. 11⅜ x 17⅞ inches (28.8 x 45.5 cm.)
Provenance: T. Griffith; J. Dillon; Farnworth Collection; E. F. White; Humphrey Roberts; Sir Joseph Beecham; Arthur Frisk of Geneva; sold Sotheby's 29 May 1963, lot 61; Oscar and Peter Johnson 1964.
Literature: Sir Walter Armstrong, *Turner*, 1902, p. 254; W. G. Rawlinson, *The Engraved Work of J. M. W. Turner R.A.*, vol. I, 1908, p. 141; vol. II, 1913, p. 194; A. J. Finberg, *Life of J. M. W. Turner R.A.*, 1961, nos. 339, 416.
Engraved: By J. Horsburgh, 1831, in the *England and Wales* series.
Exhibited: Egyptian Hall, Piccadilly, 1829; Messrs. Moon, Boys & Graves Gallery, 1833; Royal Academy, *Old Masters*, 1887, no. 66.

Drawn *circa* 1829. In 1826 Turner began work on his most ambitious series for engraving: the *Picturesque Views in England and Wales*, which was to consist of 120 plates, published in serial form. According to Rawlinson, Turner received sixty or seventy guineas for each drawing, many of which are magnificent examples of his highly wrought style, although a few are spoiled by overobtrusive figures. The first twelve subjects were published in 1827. By 1838 ninety-five plates had been issued, but despite their superb quality, the venture was financially an utter failure, possibly because the public felt they had seen enough Turner prints during the past twenty years. The original publisher, Charles Heath, went bankrupt, and in 1838 the plates together with the large number of unsold prints were put up for auction. Turner surprised everyone by appearing on the morning of the sale and buying the whole lot at the reserve price of £3,000 before it was auctioned. It was still in his possession at his death and the prints were later sold at Christie's in 1873, the plates having been broken up for the sale.

Note in the foreground fishermen digging up kegs of spirits, under the direction of a Revenue Officer.

107 YARMOUTH SANDS

Watercolor. 9¾ x 14¼ inches (24.7 x 36 cm.)

Provenance: J. Hamilton Houldsworth; G. F. Sullivan; sold Sotheby's 26 July 1961, lot 118; Colnaghi 1961.

Literature: Sir Walter Armstrong, *Turner*, 1902, p. 286.

Exhibited: Glasgow, *International Exhibition*, 1901; National Gallery, Washington, 1962, no. 90; V.M.F.A., Richmond, 1963, no. 144; Colnaghi, 1964–65, and Yale University Art Gallery, 1965, no. 36 (ill.); Victoria, 1971, no. 45.

Circa 1835. All his life Turner was fascinated by the sea which he painted again and again in all its changing moods in both oil and watercolor. He transformed marine painting in England, which, during the eighteenth century, had remained an enfeebled version of the Dutch seventeenth-century tradition.

Here Turner depicts a favorite theme: man battling against Nature in her most turbulent mood, in a scene which might almost serve to illustrate Dickens' famous description of the storm off Yarmouth in *David Copperfield* (1849–50).

108 VENICE: THE MOUTH OF THE GRAND CANAL

Watercolor. 8¼ x 12¼ inches (21 x 31 cm.)

Provenance: Rt. Hon. W. H. Smith; Sir Joseph Beecham, sold Christie's 4 May 1917; Walter H. Jones; Gilbert Davis; Colnaghi 1966.

Literature: Sir Walter Armstrong, *Turner*, 1902, p. 282; A. J. Finberg, *Early English Water-colour Drawings*, *The Studio*, 1919, p. 20, pl. xxiii; A. J. Finberg, *Turner in Venice*, 1930, p. 161.

Exhibited: Royal Academy, *British Art*, 1934, no. 899; Agnew, *Centenary of Water-colour Drawings by J. M. W. Turner*, 1951, no. 93; Arts Council, *Water-colours from the Collection of Gilbert Davis*, 1949, no. 33; British Council, *English Water-colours for Switzerland*, 1955–56, no. 123; Victoria, 1971, no. 44, pl. 10.

Turner visited Venice three or four times, the last occasion being in 1840. The dating of his later Venetian watercolors is far from easy, but this drawing was probably done during the 1840 visit. It may well have been painted on the spot, as Ruskin suggested in the case of three drawings, similar in size and closely related in style, that he owned and gave to the Ashmolean Museum, Oxford, in 1861.

Venice inspired some of Turner's most magical drawings; they appear, to borrow a phrase of Constable's, to be painted "in tinted steam."

Samuel Daniell (1775–1811)

Samuel Daniell was born at Chertsey, Surrey, brother to William and nephew to Thomas, in that family of artists. Thomas Medland was his drawing-master at the East India College, Hertford. He exhibited six times at the Royal Academy from 1792 to 1805. In December 1799, having left England as being too uneventful, he arrived at the Cape of Good Hope. For a short time he was attached to the Governor's staff, promoted from a draughtsman to an Under Secretary, until an action of his over a drawing was used as a reason for a quarrel between two socially important ladies of the colony. Daniell had to leave his post in consequence. The dismissal served him well, however, as he was appointed by Lieut.-General Dundas (whose wife was one of the adversaries) as secretary-draughtsman to a mission to Bechuanaland. It proved to be an arduous expedition covering 700 miles with inadequate transport and labor. At one point Daniell with a companion left in search of a hippopotamus, first to kill (as those he had seen would not keep still) and then to draw; but both men were lost for a few days without food and protection, and only accidental rescue saved them. He made an abundance of drawings covering life, scenery, and wildlife in Africa which, after he had returned to England in 1803, he used for his own publication, *African Scenery and Animals*, as well as for illustrations for relevant works by other authors. *African Animals* was the title of his exhibit at the Royal Academy in 1804.

Daniell left England again in 1805 for Ceylon, and from there was soon sending drawings home for his brother William to aquatint. Twelve of these drawings appeared in folio form, *A Picturesque Illustration of the Scenery, Animals and Native Inhabitants of the Island of Ceylon*, aquatints of supreme quality. In his remaining years in Ceylon, Daniell developed into a likable eccentric, known all over the island as "Sam." He ranged the jungles sketching animals with which, it is said, he was on such good terms that they stood still to be sketched, unlike his African hippopotamus. In spite of this Eden-like existence, the thirty-six-year-old Daniell succumbed to a very short illness and died in December 1811.

109 A LANDSCAPE IN CEYLON, WITH BARKING DEER AND FAWN AND A PAIR OF PARADISE FLY-CATCHERS
Watercolor. 12$\frac{15}{16}$ x 17¾ inches (32.7 x 45.1 cm.)
Provenance: L. G. Duke (D.2764), sold Sotheby's 29 April 1971, lot 51; John Baskett 1971.

John Constable, R.A. (1776–1837)

Constable was born at East Bergholt, Suffolk, on 11 June 1776, the second son of Golding Constable, a prosperous millowner. Constable's father owned water mills at Dedham and Flatford, and a windmill and roundhouse near East Bergholt. His success led him to build a substantial Georgian house next to the church at East Bergholt, and it was here that the artist was born.

Constable was not a scholar. Shortly after he left school he wrote to his father, "I found that I deserved all the reproof you was so good as to give me; and moreover I should not think you was my friend if you did not give it when you see it is necessary as it certainly then was." He had, however, from childhood an intense feeling for his natural surroundings, and wrote in later years, "The sound of water escaping from milldams etc., willows, rotten planks, shiny posts and brickwork—I love such things. Painting is with me but another word for feeling and I associate my 'careless boyhood' with all that lies on the banks of the river Stour." The artist formed several associations in his youth, the most important of which was with Sir George Beaumont, a man of refined eclecticism, the excellence of whose taste can be measured by the fact that his collection of Old Master paintings helped form, with the Angerstein pictures, the nucleus of the National Collection.

Constable's family were reluctant to see him launched on a financially hazardous career but in 1799 he was admitted to the Royal Academy schools on the recommendation of Joseph Farington, and enrolled as a student the following year.

In the first decade of the nineteenth century he pursued a number of false trails, executing portraits of farmers and their wives in the vicinity of East Bergholt, painting rather feeble altarpieces for the churches at Brantham and Nayland, and making copies for Lord Dysart of family portraits by Reynolds and Hoppner. From about the age of twenty-five he gradually developed his facility for landscape painting.

Constable's visit to the Lake District, undertaken at the suggestion of his uncle, David Pike Watts, produced a number of broadly washed, low-toned watercolors. He found no inspiration from the somberness of the overshadowing heights, and wrote to Leslie that "the solitude of the mountains" oppressed his spirits. But by 1813 and 1814 he was making beautiful little pencil sketches in the locality of Dedham Vale, in the sweeping landscape of his native county. He used them many years later as a storehouse of imagery in painting the pictures which made this part of the English countryside so closely connected with his name.

In 1816 Constable married Maria Bicknell, daughter of the Solicitor to the Admiralty. The engagement had lasted some five years and had been marked by several difficulties, the most serious of which was the Bicknells' desire not to antagonize Maria's grandfather, the wealthy Rev. Dr. Rhudde, Rector of East Bergholt, who did not care for the thought of his granddaughter marrying an impoverished artist.

In the early 1820's Constable sketched at Hampstead, where he took a house for his family in the summer months, and from 1822 he worked during the winter in the house in Charlotte Street which he had taken over after Farington's death. In 1824 Constable exhibited *The Hay Wain, A Lock on the Stour*, and a *Hampstead Heath* at the Salon in Paris. In the same year he sent his wife and children to Brighton, as Maria was showing early symptoms of the tuberculosis from which she was to die in 1828. Constable had been elected to Associate Membership of the Royal Academy in 1819 and was made a full Member in 1829, on his fourth attempt, at the age of fifty-three. He had to listen to a patronizing lecture from Lawrence, the President, and later wrote to C. R. Leslie that he was still "smarting" under his election.

Much of the latter end of Constable's life was spent working on his *English Landscape Scenery*, a volume of mezzotints engraved by David Lucas after his pictures. He died suddenly at the age of sixty on 31 March 1837.

Constable's importance as a watercolorist was undervalued until, in 1888, his daughter gave a large collection of his drawings to the Victoria and Albert Museum. Appraisal of his work in pencil and color since that time shows it to contain studies of atmospheric effect vital to his oil painting.

110 LANDSCAPE AT EAST BERGHOLT
Watercolor. 7 x 8½ inches (17.7 x 21.5 cm.)
Inscribed: Verso *East Bergholt*, in two different hands, once in pencil, once in ink, and, in a later hand, *J.C.*; figures *13* lower right in pencil.
Provenance: Dr. H. A. C. Gregory, M.C.; Agnew 1969.
Exhibited: Arts Council, *Sketches & Drawings by John Constable from the Collection of Dr. H. A. C. Gregory, M.C.*, 1949, no. 43, pl. II.

The drawing was exhibited in 1949 as *A View at Hampstead*. When it was recently lifted from the card on which it had been stuck for many years, the inscription on the back was revealed.

111 SKY STUDY WITH A RAINBOW
Watercolor. 7¼ x 9 inches (18.4 x 22.8 cm.)
Provenance: A. M. Constable; Maas Gallery 1964.
Exhibited: Colnaghi, 1964–65, and Yale University Art Gallery, 1965, no. 41.

The drawing is similar in treatment and composition to the oil sketch in the Victoria and Albert Museum (328—1888), which is dated July 28th 1812.

112 FULHAM CHURCH FROM ACROSS THE RIVER, 8 SEPTEMBER 1818
Pencil. 11¾ x 17½ inches (30 x 44.5 cm.)
Inscribed: *Fulham 8 Sepr 1818* in pencil lower left.
Provenance: Charles Russell; Fine Art Society 1961.

This drawing was probably made on one of Constable's short visits to join his wife on Putney Heath (see *John Constable's Correspondence*, ed. R. B. Beckett, vol. II, 1964, p. 237, n. 6). There is a drawing in the Victoria and Albert Museum made by Constable the following day, 9 September 1818, of Richmond Bridge.

113 SUMMER LANDSCAPE
Watercolor. 5 x 6¾ inches (12.5 x 17.3 cm.)
Inscribed: Verso *4098*, with illegible note.

Provenance: Hugh Constable; Agnew 1962.

Exhibited: V.M.F.A., Richmond, 1963, no. 126; Colnaghi, 1964–65, and Yale University Art Gallery, 1965, no. 42.

Circa 1820.

114 MARIA CONSTABLE (?), TOWARDS THE END OF HER LIFE

Pencil and watercolor. 6½ x 5 inches (16.5 x 12.5 cm.)

Provenance: L. G. Duke (D.491); Colnaghi 1960.

L. G. Duke's identification of the sitter, on the basis of comparison with the oil portrait in the Tate Gallery (2655), would appear to be convincing. The Tate Gallery picture is inscribed July 10th 1816, three months before Constable's wedding, but the drawing, with the worn expression in the face and graying hair, must have been made about a decade later.

115 OLD SARUM IN A STORM

Watercolor. 5⅞ x 7½ inches (15 x 19 cm.)

Inscribed: *June 1828* top right, not in the artist's hand.

Provenance: Sir Michael Sadler; Martin Hardie; Colnaghi 1963.

Exhibited: Louvre, Paris, *British Art*, 1938, no. 174; Wildenstein, *Constable Centenary*, 1937; Arts Council, *Three Centuries of British Water-colours and Drawings*, 1951, no. 25; Guildhall Art Gallery, *John Constable*, 1952, no. 6; V.M.F.A., Richmond, 1963, no. 125; Colnaghi, 1964–65, and Yale University Art Gallery, 1965, no. 39.

According to Sir Charles Holmes (*Constable and his Influence on Landscape Painting*, 1902, p. 249), the variants of this subject are based on a pencil drawing, formerly in the collections of H. P. Horne and Sir Edward Marsh, which was dated 20th July 1829. There is an oil sketch of the subject in the Victoria and Albert Museum, which, as Graham Reynolds points out, must have been in existence in the same year because of the circumstances in which a mezzotint was made after it by David Lucas. A watercolor drawing, which was almost certainly the one exhibited in the Royal Academy in 1834 (no. 481), under the title *The Mound of the City of Old Sarum, from the South* is also in the Victoria and Albert Museum. It looks as if the Mellon drawing is a preliminary study for the large exhibited drawing and therefore dates from the later period.

116 TREES IN A MEADOW

Watercolor over black chalk. 11⅜ x 9⅝ inches (29 x 24.5 cm.)

Provenance: S. Morse; Mrs. Church; Agnew 1960.

Literature: Martin Hardie, II, pl. 38.

Exhibited: National Gallery, Washington, 1962, no. 12; V.M.F.A., Richmond, 1963, no. 124 (ill.); Colnaghi, 1964–65, and Yale University Art Gallery, 1965, no. 38, pl. XIV.

The drawing would appear to have been made toward the end of the artist's life; cf. Graham Reynolds, *Catalogue of the Constable Collection in the Victoria and Albert Museum*, 1960, page 236, no. 415; page 310 dated *circa* 1833–36.

John Thirtle (1777–1839)

Thirtle was born at Norwich on 22 June 1777, the son of a shoemaker. He first practiced as a miniature painter, and after a period in London learning the trade of frame maker, carver, and gilder, set up in that business in his native town in 1800. Some Norwich school pictures are still to be found in the frames Thirtle made for them. He became a member of the Norwich Society of Artists, and exhibited there from 1805; he exhibited at the Royal Academy in 1808. Thirtle's early exhibits were semi-miniature portraits and imaginative subjects, but he came to find landscape more congenial. He was five years older than his friend John Sell Cotman, whose wife's sister he married in 1809. Thirtle died at Norwich on 30 September 1839.

Thirtle's work reveals the influence of both Crome and Cotman, the two outstanding artists of the Norwich school. From Crome Thirtle learned to find subject matter in apparently unremarkable scenes: stretches of the river, a few barges or sailing boats, or some old cottages. From Cotman he gained confidence and learned subtlety in his use of simplified shapes and delicately matched colors. On the whole, Thirtle's sketches in pure watercolor are more attractive than his highly finished work, and at their best have a very individual effect of sensitive simplicity. Some have remained very fresh in color, particularly in their soft russets and grays, or grays with wistful yellows; but Martin Hardie notes that Thirtle, like Crome, seems to have used a fugitive blue, possibly of an indigo type, whose fading has reduced many of Thirtle's once fine drawings to almost uniform tints of brown and red. Most of Thirtle's subjects are drawn from Norwich and its surrounding country.

117 LANDSCAPE, POSSIBLY NEAR GUILDFORD, SURREY

Watercolor. 7 x 19¼ inches (18 x 49 cm.)

Provenance: L. G. Duke (D.3074); Colnaghi 1960.

Exhibited: National Gallery, Washington, 1962, no. 83; V.M.F.A., Richmond, 1963, no. 172; Colnaghi, 1964–65, and Yale University Art Gallery, 1965, no. 46.

John Varley (1778–1842)

John Varley was born in London on 17 August 1778, the son of Richard Varley and elder brother of the artists Cornelius Varley and William Fleetwood Varley. At the age of fifteen, earning his keep as errand boy, he went to J. C. Barrow's evening drawing school, where Francia was assistant master. At twenty, he exhibited for the first time (at the Royal Academy), and soon afterwards joined the Monro circle. Through Monro Varley met discriminating patrons, and began to take pupils. From 1802 to 1804 he was a member of the Sketching Club which had been founded by Girtin and continued by Cotman. In 1804 he was a founder-member of the Water-colour Society, showing forty-one drawings in its first exhibition, and producing large batches of exhibits (termed by his fellow-artists "Varley's hot rolls") for the next forty years.

By 1804 Varley was regarded as one of the leading watercolor artists in London, and one of the most stimulating teachers. To his house (board, lodging, and tuition £100 per annum) came a steady stream of young artists, including John Linnell, Turner of Oxford, W. H. Hunt, Copley Fielding, and F. O. Finch, each of whom he encouraged to develop an individual style. Through his instructional treatises (of which he published several) Varley exerted a formative influence on countless amateurs; and some of his characteristic remarks were widely circulated, such as "Nature wants cooking" or "Every picture ought to have a *look-there*."

Varley's early drawings have a charming simplicity and directness. Subdued in coloring and revealing fine draughtsmanship, they reflect Girtin's powerful influence. Later, he became preoccupied with "compositions," ordering the ingredients of landscape into formal and often repetitive designs. Yet even when wanting in inspiration, little of his work is commonplace, for Varley remained throughout a master craftsman, with a fine sense of color and an unrivaled skill in laying in clean, luminous washes. He used to tell his pupils that flat washes of color in a good lay-in are like silences, for as every whisper can be distinctly heard in a silence, so every lighter or darker touch in a simple and masterly lay-in told at once, and was seen to be good or bad.

Varley was a warm-hearted, generous, and ebullient character. He was known to his friends as "the astrologer," because of his uncanny powers of prediction, chiefly through the casting of horoscopes. His former pupil Linnell introduced him, about 1818, to William Blake. Varley was at once excited by the older man's visionary powers, and encouraged him to make sketches of spirits. Mundane matters perplexed Varley; he was quite incapable of managing his financial affairs, and was much harassed by debtors. "All these troubles are necessary to me," he assured Linnell. "If it were not for my troubles I should burst for joy." He died in London on 17 November 1842.

118 CONWAY, NORTH WALES, 1803
Watercolor. 8¼ x 11⅝ inches (20.7 x 29.5 cm.)
Inscribed: *J. Varley / 1803* lower left; verso *Conway N. Wales J. Varley 1803.*
Provenance: John Baskett 1970.

119 HARLECH CASTLE AND TWGWYN FERRY, 1804
Watercolor. 15⅝ x 20¼ inches (39.2 x 51.5 cm.)
Inscribed: *J. Varley 1804* lower left, and, verso, in a later hand, *Tegwin ferry & Harlech Castle N. Wales / by J. Varley, 1804.*
Provenance: Agnew 1962.
Exhibited: Colnaghi, 1964–65, and Yale University Art Gallery, 1965, no. 77; Victoria, 1971, no. 47.

Cornelius Varley (1781–1873)

Cornelius Varley, younger brother of John Varley, was born in London on 21 November 1781. He was trained as a maker of scientific instruments by his uncle, Samuel Varley, a watchmaker and experimental scientist. Science remained Cornelius Varley's major interest throughout his long life. Versatile and ingenious, he designed delicate tools for making lenses, improved the construction of microscopes, studied the circulation of sap in water plants, partook in the construction of the first soda-water apparatus, and experimented in electricity. He became a Fellow of the Society of Arts in 1814. He was related by marriage to Faraday, and three of his sons became distinguished scientists.

As a young man, Cornelius Varley developed his natural talent for drawing by studying at Dr. Monro's house and on sketching tours with his brother John and with Joshua Cristall. He may at this time have contemplated art as a profession; certainly by 1804 he was sufficiently advanced as an artist to join his brother as one of the founders of the Water-colour Society (for which he wrote an anthem, to be sung to the tune of *La Marseillaise*, with the refrain "Paint on! paint on! all hearts resolved / On poetry and grace"). He was a member of the Sketching Society formed by the Chalon brothers and others, with the official title of "The Society for the Study of Epic and Pastoral Design"; their subjects were chosen from classical and literary themes, usually executed in monochrome, and Cornelius Varley's were notably Cotmanesque in treatment. He exhibited at the Water-colour Society from 1805 to 1820 and at the Royal Academy from 1803 to 1859. Meanwhile, he had invented, for the use of artists drawing portraits, landscape, and architectural subjects, the Graphic Telescope (patented 5 April 1811), which projected an image flat upon paper, to be traced round. Cornelius and John Varley often (though by no means invariably) made use of the Graphic Telescope; but Cotman, though he took one with his sketching equipment to Normandy, found it too cumbersome for regular use.

Cornelius Varley was a less prolific but more sensitive artist than his brother. He was particularly interested in trying to portray skies and the movement of trees; in general, however, his art has more imagination than analysis in it. His palette was delicate but never insipid. He worked in quiet tones, preferably dovelike grays, adding subtle touches of color to produce an effect which Iolo Williams calls "melodious and rippling."

A small, cherubic-faced man, enthusiastic, eccentric and amiable, Cornelius Varley died in London on 2 October 1873.

120 "LLYN TALLY LLIN AT MY BACK"

Watercolor. 19½ x 25 inches (49.5 x 63.4 cm.)

Inscribed: *Llyn Tally Llin at my back Corn' Varley* in margin below drawing.

Provenance: Maas Gallery 1967.

Literature: Martin Hardie, II, pl. 91; Dudley Snelgrove, *Drawings and Water-colours in the Collection of Mr. and Mrs. Paul Mellon*, Old Water-colour Society's Club, vol. XLIII, 1968, pl. VII.

Exhibited: Victoria, 1971, no. 46, pl. 11.

John Sell Cotman (1782–1842)

Cotman was born on 16 May 1782 at Norwich, the son of a silk mercer. He taught himself to draw by copying prints; three of his juvenile drawings from caricature prints are in the Mellon collection. At the age of sixteen he went to London and found brief employment coloring prints for Ackermann's Repository of Arts. Like many young artists of that time, he gravitated to Dr. Monro's house to copy drawings in the doctor's valuable collection. He joined Girtin's Sketching Society, and much of his early work has a strong Girtin flavor. His exhibits at the Royal Academy each year between 1800 and 1806 were from tours made in Surrey, Wales, and Yorkshire, each group of drawings exhibited showing a progression toward the characteristic manner in which he painted the inspired watercolors at and about Rokeby Park on the Greta in Yorkshire. He never surpassed these, but, because contemporary connoisseurs found them unconventional and unacceptable, Cotman returned to his native Norwich in 1806. Temporarily discouraged in his work in watercolor he turned to painting in oil. At this time he instituted a "Circulating Library" of some 350 of his own drawing compositions for students to copy as exercises.

Cotman became a member, and eventually the President, of the newly founded Norwich Society of Artists. He married in 1809 and the following year began a major series of etchings of antiquarian remains in Norfolk: "sorry drudgery, and only calculated for money-making," he declared. His studies of ancient churches and castles rewarded him, if not with financial success, with a feeling for the texture of stonework which, particularly when translated into watercolor, gives his buildings solidity and strength. In 1812 he left Norwich to settle in Yarmouth at the invitation of Dawson Turner, a banker, botanist, and active antiquary. Cotman made three visits to Normandy during 1817 and 1820 at Dawson Turner's instigation, and sketches he made there provided him with subject matter for years to come. He moved back to Norwich in 1823 and tried to launch a new drawing school by making a sale of over 200 of his drawings in London, but they netted only the meager sum of £165. By temperament Cotman was prone to alternating moods of extravagant hope and black despair; he now found himself sinking under "hopelessness." He may have been cheered by his election to Associate Membership of the Water-colour Society in London, and by a visit from his old friend John Varley, artist, astrologer, and cheerful extrovert, who on finding Cotman ill and gloomily contemplating death declared (and was only nine months out in his prediction): "Impossible! no such thing! I tell you there are twenty years for you yet to come!" In 1834 Cotman was appointed Drawing Master to the newly established King's College, London; but financial difficulties continued to dog him. A last visit to Norfolk gave him a brief, happy burst of activity, during which he exclaimed: " 'tis as impossible to pass a fine subject and not to book it as it is for a miser to pass a guinea and not pick it up." He died the following year in London, on 24 July 1842.

121 ABERYSTWYTH CASTLE

Watercolor. 11⅜ x 19⅝ inches (28.9 x 49.9 cm.), on contemporary bordered mount.

Inscribed: *J. S. Cotman* lower right, and inscribed on verso *Aberiwith* in pencil.

Provenance: George Bissill 1969.

This drawing was made during Cotman's first tour of Wales in 1800; a sketch of this castle dated 18 July 1800 is in the British Museum. The tonal depth and intensity are characteristic of Cotman's drawings at this time, and it is particularly comparable to the dramatic *St. Mary Redcliffe, Bristol* in the British Museum (L.B., I., no. 9).

122 IN ROKEBY PARK

Watercolor. 13 x 19 inches (33 x 22.9 cm.)
Provenance: Lewis G. Fry; Anthony Fry; Agnew 1971.
Literature: S. D. Kitson, *The Life of John Sell Cotman*, 1937, p. 82.
Exhibited: Tate Gallery, *Cotman*, 1922, no. 22; Royal Society of British Artists, *Centenary Exhibition*, 1923, no. 23.

In the summer of 1805 Cotman was staying at Rokeby Park at the invitation of John Morritt, traveler and Greek scholar. He refers in a letter to Dawson Turner to making drawings "coloured from Nature and close copies of that ficle [sic] Dame." Of these outstanding watercolors done in this part of Yorkshire, most were, according to Martin Hardie, "studied, balanced and arranged in the studio." This drawing of the woods, however, has the feeling of freedom and directness, and, accepting that blue was the fashionable color among watercolorists of that day, it is most likely a *plein air* painting.

123 DOMFRONT, LOOKING TO THE SOUTH EAST

Pencil and brown wash. Subject: 10¼ x 16⅛ inches (26 x 40.8 cm.). Paper: 11⅛ x 16½ inches (28.3 x 42.1 cm.)
Inscribed: *J. S. Cotman* and *Domfront looking South East* in pencil on margin at base.
Provenance: Walter Gurney, sold Sotheby's 10 April 1933, lot 26; Martin Hardie; Colnaghi 1961.
Literature: H. Isherwood Kay, *J. S. Cotman's Letters from Normandy 1817–1820*, Walpole Society, 1926, vol. xiv, p. 87; Vasari Society, 2nd Series, 1933, xiv, 8.
Exhibited: Royal Academy, *British Art*, 1934, no. 822, pl. CLXXIX; Bucharest, *British Drawings*, 1935–36; Paris, *British Painting*, 1938, no. 225; British Council, Scandinavia, *British Painting 1730–1850*, 1949–50, no. 23; Arts Council, *Three Centuries of British Water-colours and Drawings*, 1951, no. 38; National Gallery, Washington, 1962, no. 17a; V.M.F.A., Richmond, 1963, no. 174 (ill.); Colnaghi, 1964–65, and Yale University Art Gallery, 1965, no. 45 (ill.).

Cotman was at Domfront during his third visit to Normandy in 1820. It is not surprising that he delayed, at least for a short time, his mission to draw architecture when confronted with this array of rock scenery. He was always moved to draw stone, whether in its natural mass state or hewn and shaped into buildings; this is evident in so much of his work. A similar drawing is in the City Art Gallery, Leeds.

124 DOORWAY AND WINDOW OF A CHURCH

Watercolor. 12⅞ x 9⅜ inches (32.7 x 23.8 cm.)
Provenance: Maas Gallery 1966.
Literature: Dudley Snelgrove, *Drawings and Water-colours in the Collection of Mr. and Mrs. Paul Mellon*, Old Water-colour Society's Club, vol. XLIII, 1968, p. 22, pl. IX.

Exhibited: Victoria, 1971, no. 4.

The church or cathedral to which this subject belongs has not yet been identified. It was drawn, probably, when Cotman was collecting subjects for his etchings for *Specimens of Norman and Gothic Architecture in Norfolk*, published in 1817.

Sydney D. Kitson, Cotman's biographer, collected a considerable number of his architectural drawings which are now in the Mellon collection.

David Cox (1783–1859)

Cox was born in Birmingham on 29 April 1783. His father, a blacksmith, apprenticed him to the "toy trade," where Cox painted in miniature on lockets and trinkets. His scale of work increased to that of scene-painting for the Birmingham Theatre Royal, and while doing this he had lessons from Joseph Barber at night school. In 1804 he continued this routine in London, painting scenery for Astley's Theatre and becoming a pupil of John Varley, and exhibiting the following year at the Royal Academy. Shortly after he married, he lived in Dulwich and set up as a drawing-master, but a later appointment in this role at Farnham Military College proved a failure, Cox not liking the work, the exalted rank of captain, or being separated from his family. He was more successful when he was teaching at Hereford from 1815 to 1817. During this period he published several books on painting, which went into numerous editions. Cox made visits to Holland, Belgium, and France, producing in the latter place some of his best work. When he was fifty-eight he moved to Harborne, near his birthplace, and died there on 7 June 1859. Cox was a well-loved, industrious man of a genial disposition which moved Turner to call him "Farmer Cox."

"There is no straining after elegant formalities, no precise insistence upon particular rules of composition, no substitution of convention for direct inspiration," is an excellent assessment by A. L. Baldry of Cox's work. After his early years, when Varley's conventions dominated, Cox's methods changed little, and he found his own characteristic touch, that of dappling in colors as lightly as fallen leaves. Nature and atmosphere were the essence of his drawings, whether of town streets, Welsh hills, or wind-blown shores. He rarely experimented, but in 1804 he found a sheet of wrapping paper with a rough, absorbent surface which was exciting and satisfying to paint on, and ordered a large quantity. Some drawings have the paper's excise stamp on their backs. Later, a similar paper was manufactured purposely for watercolorists, and given the trade name "David Cox paper."

125 ON LANCASTER SANDS, LOW TIDE
Watercolor. 10⅛ x 14½ inches (25.7 x 36.8 cm.)
Provenance: Martin Hardie; Colnaghi 1961.
Literature: Martin Hardie, II, p. 202, pl. 189.
Exhibited: Arts Council, *Three Centuries of British Water-colours and Drawings*, 1951, no. 42; Paris, *English Landscape Painting*, 1953, no. 32; U.S.A., *Masters of British Painting*, 1956–67, no. 31; V.M.F.A., Richmond, 1963, no. 178; Colnaghi, 1964–65, and Yale University Art Gallery, 1965, no. 43 (ill.); Victoria, 1971, no. 8.

Peter De Wint (1784–1849)

De Wint was born on 21 January 1784 at Stone in Staffordshire. His father was born in New York, practiced as a doctor in Stone, and intended his son to follow in that profession. De Wint's inclination was for art, however, and he studied under John Raphael Smith, the engraver and portrait draughtsman. He was a fellow-pupil and constant friend of William Hilton (later Royal Academician) whose sister he married. From 1809 he studied at the Royal Academy schools, exhibiting at the Academy from that year until 1828. For about forty years he exhibited at the Water-colour Society as a member. De Wint's association with John Varley and with Dr. Monro's celebrated circle of artists provided all the atmosphere and inspiration needed to nourish his talent for watercolor. His individual method of coloring evolved in the use of mature warm tones, which produced an effective richness rarely achieved by his imitators; but as a draughtsman he had many peers. Travel abroad had no appeal to him after a single visit to Normandy, and his main work was done in the northern counties of England. He became a successful teacher to cultured amateurs, none of whom progressed to an independent style.

De Wint was a religious man, and although reputed in his family to have an edgy temper, made and kept many friends throughout his life. He died in London on 30 June 1849 and is buried with his brother-in-law in the Chapel Royal of the Savoy.

126 THE OLD BRIDGE

Watercolor. 11¼ x 9¾ inches (28.5 x 24.7 cm.)

Provenance: Mrs. Tatlock, the artist's daughter; Miss Bostock; Frank H. Fulford; Dr. N. Bartman; Agnew 1962.

Exhibited: Usher Art Gallery, Lincoln, *Peter De Wint*, 1937, no. 124; Victoria, 1971, no. 14.

127 THE FOSS DYKE NEAR LINCOLN

Watercolor. 9¾ x 16½ inches (24.7 x 42 cm.)

Provenance: Mrs. Frank Howarth; Agnew 1962.

Literature: Martin Hardie, II, pl. 198.

Exhibited: V.M.F.A., Richmond, 1963, no. 179; Colnaghi, 1964–65, and Yale University Art Gallery, 1965, no. 49.

Sir David Wilkie, R. A. (1785–1841)

Wilkie was born the son of a Scottish minister at Cults, Fifeshire, on 18 November 1785. Despite early family wishes that he should follow his father in the Ministry, he entered the Trustees' Academy in Edinburgh at the age of fourteen in 1799, and worked there for four years under John Graham. His years of study were followed by a short stay at home, during which time he painted his first picture *Pitlessie Fair* and executed a few portraits and miniatures. In 1805 he traveled by sea from Leith, just outside Edinburgh, to London and entered the Royal Academy schools as a student. The following year he exhibited *The Village Politicians*, the first of one hundred pictures that he showed at the Academy between 1806 and 1842. He was elected Associate of the Royal Academy in 1809 and full Member in 1811. In 1812 he held an unsuccessful exhibition in Pall Mall of twenty-nine of his own works. He returned to Scotland to see his family and then in 1814 made his first visit to the Continent, where he studied the collections in the Louvre, at that time enriched with works of art plundered by Napoleon. The following years saw the completion of *Distraining for Rent, Penny Wedding, Reading the Will*, and *Chelsea Pensioners Reading the Gazette of the Battle of Waterloo*. These pictures of a topical genre influenced by Dutch seventeenth-century painting, provided Wilkie with his special reputation. In 1825 Wilkie again set out for Paris, and traveled on to Florence and thence to Rome, Naples, Bologna, Venice, Dresden, Prague, and Vienna. Traveling home the following year after a winter in Italy, he changed his mind in Geneva and went to Madrid, where he arrived in October 1827, getting back to London in the spring of 1828. A number of dramatic subjects resulted from his stay in Spain including the *The Guerilla Council of War, The Guerilla taking leave of his Confessor, The Maid of Saragossa*, and *The Confessional*, but they were not greeted with the same public approval that his earlier domestic scenes had received. Wilkie was appointed Painter-in-Ordinary by George IV and was knighted by William IV in 1836. In 1840, he left England once again on a journey to the Middle East. He reached Istanbul in October and then visited Smyrna, Beirut, and Jerusalem. He traveled back via Alexandria and Malta. In Malta he became seriously ill, apparently from food poisoning and died as the vessel which was bearing him left the harbor. He was buried at sea on the same day, 1 June 1841, in his fifty-sixth year.

128 A GIRL, THREE-QUARTER LENGTH, WEARING A LARGE HAT

Pen and ink and brown wash. 12¼ x 8½ inches (31 x 21.5 cm.)
Inscribed: D. W. top right.
Provenance: Randall Davies; T. E. Lowinsky (Lugt 2420a); Justin Lowinsky 1963.
Exhibited: Royal Academy, *British Art*, 1934, no. 863 (as *A Standing Woman*).

Anthony Vandyke Copley Fielding (1787–1855)

Copley Fielding (as he has invariably been known, originally no doubt to distinguish him among a family of painters) was born at East Sowerby, Yorkshire, in 1787. His father, a portrait painter and friend of John Singleton Copley, R.A., instructed the boy and his three brothers in painting. In 1809 Copley Fielding moved to London, and lived near John Varley, whose sister-in-law he married. Varley (though not his teacher) gave him friendly advice, and in 1810 he was elected an Associate of the Water-colour Society. Within a few years he had embarked on what has fairly been called "his stupendous traffic in drawings": exhibits averaging forty a year over forty-three years, and totaling 1,748. He was closely involved with the administration of the Society, as Treasurer, Secretary, Vice-President and, on Cristall's retirement, President from 1831 until his death at Worthing on 3 March 1855.

Copley Fielding's work was popular, prolific, and (not surprisingly, given his huge output) repetitive. His favorite themes, drawn from numerous tours of the Lake District and Wales and long residence on the coast, were moorland, downland, and seascape; his preferred atmosphere was that misty gleam which Ruskin so admired in his work. Compared with the work in landscape which Cox and De Wint were producing in the same period, his art seems a little commonplace; however, his suave handling of watercolor found readier patrons than Cox's rough and brusque manner or De Wint's boldness. A best seller in his own day is apt to forfeit sympathy in the next. It needs almost an effort of will to recognize that while Copley Fielding may not startle us by originality, he was a sound and, after all, unpretentious craftsman whose chief appeal, in Martin Hardie's words, is "a certain timelessness, as if the hot stillness had hung for centuries over the scene."

129 A VIEW OF SNOWDON FROM THE SANDS OF TRAETH MAWR TAKEN AT THE FORD BETWEEN PONT ABERGLASLYN AND TREMADOC, 1834
Watercolor. 25 x 35¾ inches (63.5 x 90.7 cm.)
Inscribed: *Copley Fielding 1834* lower right.
Provenance: Polak 1968.
Exhibited: Old Water-colour Society, 1834, no. 93.

William Turner (of Oxford) (1789–1862)

Turner of Oxford (invariably so-called, to distinguish him from his great contemporary, J. M. W. Turner) was born at Black Bourton, Oxfordshire, on 12 November 1789. He was one of John Varley's first and most promising pupils, producing early work which moved the enthusiastic Varley to speak "violently" of his merits, and earned him the distinction of election to full membership of the Old Water-colour Society in 1808, a few weeks after his nineteenth birthday. His brilliance, however, was short-lived; the dramatic intensity of his early landscapes gave way to a painstaking realism, depending for effect on calculated color and fidelity of detail. But if he was unoriginal, he was unpretentious, and often very pleasing; Ruskin praised the "quiet and simple earnestness" of "this patient and unassuming artist." A prolific and indefatigable worker, Turner of Oxford exhibited annually at the Old Water-colour Society for over fifty years, but as a "country member," for he left London about 1811 and spent the rest of his long life (apart from many sketching tours) in Oxford. There he had "numerous pupils . . . both in and out of the University"; no notable watercolorists are among them, perhaps because although his teaching methods were characteristically practical and systematic, he lacked the inspirational genius of his own master. He died in Oxford on 7 August 1862.

130 DONATI'S COMET, OXFORD, 7.30 P.M., 5 OCTOBER 1858
Watercolor. 10⅛ x 14⅜ inches (25.8 x 36.7 cm.)
Inscribed: 'W. Turner / Oxford' lower right (dated in detail on an old mount, now lost).
Provenance: Colnaghi 1965.

On the evening of 5 October 1858, reported the *Annual Register*, "the population of all the western world was probably out of doors gazing on the phenomenon" of one of the century's most spectacular comets. Now known as Donati's comet, because first perceived by M. Donati, astronomer at the museum of Florence, on 2 June 1858, it had been visible to the naked eye for almost a month before 5 October, when it was at its brightest. That evening was "very fine," and the comet's appearance "extremely magnificent. The nucleus or head resembled a globe of light clothed in several envelopes of lesser light. The outermost of these envelopes was continued indefinitely to the northward in two bands, with a lesser light in between, forming the tail." Even nowadays, remarked *The Times* that week, when the solar system is so familiar that ladies' maids understand it as easily as needlework or clear-starching, the spectacle of a comet remains awe-inspiring.

The comet presented a subject of particular appeal to Turner of Oxford. The sky plays a vital part in many of his drawings, and he devoted much intent study to portraying atmospheric changes, often adding to the titles of his drawings such descriptions as "twilight," "storm clearing off," "after rain," or "sunrise." The comet's long visibility provided the chance to compose and meditate upon his scene in advance, and in particular to work out the degrees of color needed to portray the uncanny light over the still landscape. The scene is finished with his customary carefulness, and with his characteristically intense coloring.

John Martin (1789–1854)

Martin was born on 19 July 1789 at Haydon Bridge in the Tyne Valley, the thirteenth child of poverty-stricken parents. After a brief apprenticeship to a coach painter, he became the pupil of Boniface Musso, an Italian drawing-master in Newcastle; and in 1806, at the age of seventeen, went with Musso and his family to live in London. For the next six years he was employed painting in enamel on china and glass (an art he learned from Musso's son, Charles Muss), meanwhile studying perspective and architecture, and making watercolors and small oil paintings. His *Landscape, A Composition* was exhibited at the Royal Academy in 1811.

The following year Martin exhibited what he called "my *first* work," *Sadak in Search of the Waters of Oblivion*—the first, that is, of a series of luridly colored canvases depicting doom-laden episodes from the Bible, filled with hordes of frantic figures and stupendous dream architecture, shot through with supernatural flashes of light. *Joshua Commanding the Sun to Stand Still, Belshazzar's Feast, The Deluge, The Fall of Babylon, The Fall of Nineveh*, and *Pandemonium* created popular sensations when exhibited at the Royal Academy or the British Institution, and sold well, as did Martin's own mezzotints after them; and in 1823 he received £2,000 for his designs for *Paradise Lost*. He had, however, many harsh critics. Charles Lamb deplored his "phantasmagoric tricks," Hazlitt declared that "he wearies the imagination instead of exciting it," and Ruskin derided his works as "as much makeable to order as a tea-tray or a coal-scuttle."

Martin's imagery, Francis Klingender suggests, was inspired by the great engineering works of the Industrial Revolution; "he gave Hell the image of industry." Martin himself had a strong inventive streak, and published numerous plans for bringing a supply of pure water to London, disposing of its sewage, constructing iron ships and preventing accidents in mines. He was a small, energetic man, handsome in appearance and enthusiastic in religion. He died at Douglas in the Isle of Man on 17 February 1854.

Martin used sepia wash for small biblical studies, and watercolor for comparatively realistic landscapes, often drawn from nature on his excursions in search of sources of pure water for London. Even in the gentle medium of watercolor, his coloring is stunning rather than subtle; there is often storm in the air, even if not directly invoked by divine retribution.

131 THE BANKS OF THE THAMES, OPPOSITE POPE'S VILLA, 1850
Watercolor and body color on brown paper. 11¾ x 23⅝ inches (30 x 60 cm.)
Inscribed: *J. Martin 1850* lower left.
Provenance: Colnaghi 1963.

William Henry Hunt (1790–1864)

Hunt was born in London on 28 March 1790, the son of a tinplate worker. He suffered from a deformity in his legs, and according to an uncle, "was always a cripple, and as he was fit for nothing, they made an artist of him." His father, unenthusiastic about the profession but sound in his choice of teacher, apprenticed the boy to John Varley. In 1808 he joined the Royal Academy schools, exhibiting at the Royal Academy from 1807 to 1811. He exhibited extensively at the Water-colour Society from 1814 for fifty years.

As a young man, Hunt was employed by the Duke of Devonshire and the Earl of Essex to make drawings of rooms in their houses. At the Earl's home at Cassiobury, Hunt met Dr. Monro who gave him access to his important collection of drawings. The doctor's Canalettos particularly impressed Hunt. He copied them, and through close study of Canaletto evolved his own characteristic style of drawing. Of this, *St. Martin-in-the-Fields* is an outstanding example, showing Hunt's rugged outline done in reed-pen, with flowing washes of color. Hunt made many drawings in this style, of church interiors and country scenes near Bushey, while staying with Dr. Monro. Some were done while Hunt was "trundled on a sort of barrow with a hood over it, drawn by a man or a donkey."

Hunt's method gradually changed: his line became tighter and his coloring more vivid. He turned to drawing sentimental scenes of bucolic characters coyly posing, and, more successfully, young girls occupied in sewing or reading with light softly reflected upwards on their faces. His later compositions of birds' nests, fruit, and dead animals, meticulous in technique and faithfully observed, seem to sacrifice imagination to their contrived settings.

In later years Hunt lived at Hastings, but he died in London on 10 February 1864.

Watercolor. 19½ x 13½ inches (49.5 x 34.3 cm.)

Inscribed: *W. Hunt* lower right.

Provenance: C. J. Pooley; C. A. Coutts; William Quilter; Wynn Ellis; T. Girtin; Tom Girtin; John Baskett 1970.

Literature: F. G. Stephens, *William Henry Hunt*, Old Water-colour Society's Club, vol. XII, 1935, pl. XI.

Exhibited: Fine Art Society, 1879–80, no. 123; Burlington Fine Arts Club, 1919, no. 34, pl. XV; British Empire Exhibition, Wembley, 1924; Graves Art Gallery, Sheffield, *Early Water-colours from the Collection of Thomas Girtin Jnr.*, 1953, no. 64; Leeds City Art Gallery, *Early English Water-colours*, 1958, no. 68; Royal Academy, *The Girtin Collection*, 1962, no. 50.

St. Martin-in-the-Fields, first mentioned in 1222, was several times rebuilt. The church seen here was designed by James Gibbs in 1722–26. It was hemmed in by a narrow lane until the middle of the last century, when the whole area facing it was replanned and its frontage was displayed. The church commands admiration not only for its history and high elegance but also for its crypt which has given charitable sanctuary at night for countless unfortunates. It is interesting in the context of this catalogue in that John Constable is among the many notables who was married there.

John Linnell (1792–1882)

Linnell was born on 16 June 1792 in Bloomsbury, London, the son of a frame-maker and printseller. At the age of twelve he became John Varley's pupil for two years; at fourteen he entered the Royal Academy schools, and soon became one of the Monro circle. He first exhibited at the Royal Academy in 1807, and thenceforth exhibited regularly there and at the British Institution. He was a member of the Water-colour Society from 1812 to 1820, when he resigned to concentrate on oil. Linnell was a versatile artist. His reputation rests chiefly on his landscape painting in oil, but he also painted portraits in various media (including miniatures on ivory) and made numerous drawings. His output was large; he never lacked patrons, and had a keen business sense. Linnell lived for many years at Hampstead, then at Bayswater, from where he retired in 1852 to Redhill, at which he continued to live for the next thirty years, glorifying in oils the Surrey landscape, and particularly its harvest fields. He died on 20 January 1882, in his ninetieth year.

Linnell was a self-righteous, determined, cheerful, somewhat cranky man whose sincerity in some matters has been questioned. In religion a dissenter, rejecting in turn the Anglicans, the Baptists, and the Plymouth Brethren, he claimed complete patriarchal authority over his family. Though for twenty years he put his name forward for Associate Membership of the Royal Academy, he was never elected, presumably because fellow-artists disliked either his personality or his aggressive Nonconformity; he himself alleged that his failure was due to refusal to take part in "servile electioneering," and, after withdrawing his name, came to speak of titles and distinctions as "marks of the beast." Linnell's relationships with two outstanding artists, Blake and Palmer, show him in varying lights. At a time when Blake was aging, impoverished and embittered, Linnell befriended him, introduced him to stimulating companions such as John Varley and the Shoreham circle of "Ancients," and gave him invaluable help by himself commissioning works from Blake (paying in advance for work uncompleted at Blake's death). Samuel Palmer as a young man spoke of Linnell as "a good angel from heaven" and was his eager disciple; Linnell's landscapes, especially his ripe corn-fields and what Palmer called "those glorious round clouds" stimulated Palmer's own pastoral vein. Later, however, after Palmer had married Linnell's eldest daughter Hannah, Linnell's authority over Palmer grew oppressive and damaging. The complexity of Linnell's character entitles him to fuller and possibly fairer appraisal than he has so far received.

133 LANDSCAPE IN NORTH WALES, 1813

Watercolor. 9¼ x 14½ inches (23.5 x 36.8 cm.)

Provenance: Agnew 1961.

Exhibited: National Gallery, Washington, 1962, no. 45; V.M.F.A., Richmond, 1963, no. 184.

David Roberts, R.A. (1796–1864)

Roberts was born at Stockbridge, near Edinburgh, on 2 October 1796, the son of a poor cobbler. After serving an apprenticeship with a house painter, he became scene-painter to Bannister's traveling circus, and then to theatres in Glasgow, Edinburgh, York, and London. In 1822 he was employed painting sets and backcloths at Drury Lane Theatre, in company with Clarkson Stanfield, who became his lifelong friend. Stanfield also painted scenery for his friend Charles Dickens' theatricals. Meanwhile Roberts was diligently teaching himself to draw and paint on a finer scale. He traveled extensively abroad, with highly productive results. Drawings made in Spain were published, in colored lithography, in *Picturesque Sketches in Spain during the years 1822 and 1823*. His greatest published work was *Views in the Holy Land, Syria, Idumea, Arabia, Egypt and Nubia*, published in parts from 1842 to 1849. It consisted of about 250 plates in chromo-lithography, and was acclaimed for the accuracy of its architecture and costume. It was the first pictorial work of any size to present to the public sites, scenes, and buildings of sacred places which, up till then, had been familiar in name only. The drawings for this work were expertly made, delicately colored, and free from any idiomatic contrivance.

Roberts exhibited over 100 works at the Royal Academy. In 1829 he was elected honorary member of the Royal Scottish Academy, and in 1841 Royal Academician. He was appointed one of the Commissioners for the Great Exhibition of 1851. Roberts' life is a model of one who, realizing his talents and working them hard, progressed from humble beginnings to comfortable affluence without losing integrity. He died in London on 25 November 1864.

134 KARNAC, 1838

Watercolor. 19¼ x 13 inches (49 x 33 cm.)

Inscribed: *Karnac 1838* lower left, and *David Roberts R.A. 1838* lower right.

Provenance: Spink and Son 1966.

James Holland (1799–1870)

Holland was born on 18 October 1799 at Burslem, Staffordshire. His grandfather was a pottery manufacturer; the boy learned from his grandmother and his father the art of painting flowers on pottery and porcelain, then worked for seven years' semi-apprenticeship in James Davenport's Longport factory. Coming to London in 1819, he sold flower drawings and gave lessons for a living, meanwhile teaching himself to paint landscape and architecture, Bonington's influence being clearly apparent in his early work. Holland painted occasional flower pieces throughout his life, graduating from meticulous studies to spontaneous sketches allowing full freedom for that sensitive love of color which is the most distinctive aspect of his work.

From 1831 Holland made regular visits to the Continent, finding his most congenial subject-matter in Italy, and above all in Venice, with which his name is particularly associated. He drew with great verve: swiftly, with a sure descriptive power which could suggest detail without precisely stating it. With the same light, almost fluttering touch he would add delicate washes of color, enlivened with richer tints. There was, Thackeray noted in 1840, nothing "glib or smooth" about his work. He delighted in painting water: the Thames lapping up to the façade of Greenwich Hospital, the greenish, glittering Venetian lagoons, the deep Mediterranean, or the Kentish seaside with its cheerful litter of boardinghouses and bathing-machines. Later, as he painted increasingly in oils, his use of color grew more heavy-handed (or "rapturous" as the *Art Journal* put it in 1863); and his subjects became repetitious, over-working the popular formula of tawny-pink palazzo at turquoise water's edge. Holland was elected an Associate of the Water-colour Society in 1835, resigned eight years later, probably hoping that his increasing exhibits of oils at the Royal Academy might lead to membership there, but rejoined the Water-colour Society in 1856, exhibiting in all nearly 200 works there. He died in London on 12 February 1870.

Holland was a pleasant, personable man who never lacked patrons, pupils, or friends. Martin Hardie describes a watercolor portrait of him by his friend W. H. Hunt, showing Holland at the age of twenty-eight, "dark-haired, dark-eyed, debonair, with crimson scarf and the hint of a canary waistcoat, seated negligently in front of his easel, a bit of a dandy even, in his flowered painting smock, very much the easy-going successful young artist." He had a reputation for wit, and once feelingly remarked, "Parting with a sketch is like parting with a tooth: once sold it cannot be replaced."

135 COAST SCENE WITH SAILING BOATS
Watercolor. 11½ x 17½ inches (29.2 x 44.5 cm.)
Provenance: Manning Gallery 1968.

Richard Parkes Bonington (1802–1828)

Bonington was born at Arnold near Nottingham on 25 October 1802, his father being a drawing-master and printseller, his mother mistress of a school for young ladies. Economic depression in Nottinghamshire impelled his father in 1817 to seek better fortune in France. At Calais, Bonington was accepted as a pupil of Louis Francia (then aged forty-six), who had worked in England among prominent artists, including Girtin and Cotman. Although his father opposed his study of landscape, Bonington persevered, and in 1815 went to Paris with an introduction to the twenty-one-year-old Delacroix. Between 1820 and 1822 he studied under Baron Gros at the Ecole des Beaux-Arts, in the latter year exhibiting for the first time at the Salon. Two years later his exhibits there won him a gold medal, an honor achieved that year by Constable and Copley Fielding. He did not exhibit at the Royal Academy until 1827. Meanwhile he had traveled in Flanders, Belgium, and Italy, and made several visits to England. In London in 1825, he made drawings of armor in the Samuel Meyrick collection with Delacroix, with whom he shared a studio on his return to Paris. On 23 September 1828, he died of consumption in London, his brilliant career tragically ended in his twenty-sixth year.

"He died, and fashion made him an idol," declared the *Morning Post*. Successive sales dispersed the works remaining in Bonington's studio and in his parents' hands. In these and other sales, imitations and copies appeared, some known to be by his father, and experts still exercise great caution in attribution. Martin Hardie notes a certain license with perspective in Bonington's work which, he suggests, can be a clue to distinguishing it from that of artists treating similar subjects.

Bonington's appeal is primarily as a colorist. His early work is low-toned, revealing the influence of Girtin transmitted through Francia: in his later landscapes and figure work he used color with a richness and technical skill that won him acclaim in France years before he was appreciated in England. Martin Hardie observes that "his colour notes have a resonance and translucency which in other hands might have come perilously near to crudity. What saves him from the charge of overstatement or facile picturesqueness is that he knows how to combine cold notes of grey with his warmer and more positive tones, crisp and flickering strokes with his steady washes. Bonington is a master of soft undertones."

136 LANDSCAPE WITH WINDMILLS

Watercolor. 8⅛ x 10⅝ inches (20.5 x 27 cm.)
Provenance: Mrs. E. W. Tilling; Mrs. E. Potter; Agnew 1962.
Exhibited: V.M.F.A., Richmond, 1963, no. 186.

Thomas Shotter Boys (1803–1874)

Boys was born in Pentonville, London, on 2 January 1803. He trained as an engraver from the age of fourteen and, on going to France in 1825, found steady employment in this trade. In his later years engraving and lithography became his livelihood, sadly declining to reproductive hackwork.

Boys was fortunate in having the friendship of Bonington in Paris during the last three years of Bonington's short life. He was persuaded by Bonington to paint in watercolor, and to take up lithography. Boys became equally skillful in either medium; when he combined the two, the results showed him to be a superb craftsman. In 1839 he published in chromolithography *Picturesque Architecture in Paris, Ghent, Antwerp and Rouen*, and in 1842 *Original Views of London As It Is*, perhaps his most popular series; these were colored by hand from key drawings. Among his reproductive works were several etchings and lithographs for Ruskin's *Modern Painters* and *Stones of Venice*. Boys exhibited constantly at the New Watercolour Society from 1832 to 1873, and at the Royal Academy in 1847 and 1848. He died in reduced circumstances in London on 10 October 1874.

137 L'INSTITUT DE FRANCE, PARIS
   Watercolor. 14 x 10⅞ inches (35.5 x 27.6 cm.)
   Inscribed: 'Thomas Boys / *1830*' lower center.
   Provenance: C. R. N. Routh; Agnew 1962.
   Exhibited: Paris, *Huit Siècles de Vie Britannique à Paris*, 1948, no. 579; V.M.F.A., Richmond, 1963, no. 196 (ill.); Colnaghi, 1964–65, and Yale University Art Gallery, 1965, no. 50 (ill.).

   L'Institut de France is a prime example in watercolor of the affinity between the drawings of Bonington and Boys. A third artist, William Callow, working in Paris at the same time, and friendly with both of them, also drew in this clear, refined manner and made similar compositions. Confusion in attribution is sometimes inevitable when watercolors of this quality, style, and date appear unsigned.

Samuel Palmer (1805–1881)

Samuel Palmer was born on 27 January 1805 at Newington in South London, the son of a Baptist bookseller of the same name. For a time, after the Palmers had moved to Houndsditch, young Samuel attended Merchant Taylors' School, but left at about the age of twelve or thirteen. Palmer became a pupil of the minor artist William Wate; he first exhibited at the Royal Academy in 1819 at the age of fourteen, and up to 1873 showed more than fifty items. Palmer's early work was strongly influenced by David Cox's *Treatise of Landscape Painting*. He met John Linnell in the autumn of 1822 when he was seventeen and Linnell was thirty. Linnell introduced Palmer to his former master John Varley, and in 1824 to William Blake. Blake befriended Palmer and his friends Richmond, Calvert, and Frederick Tatham. In about 1827 Palmer settled in the Kentish village of Shoreham, which he had previously visited, and lived there with his widowed father in what he was to call his "valley of vision" for seven years. He was visited there by, among others, Calvert, Richmond, and Francis Oliver Finch, who called themselves "The Ancients." Some of Palmer's most remarkable drawings were made during this period.

Martin Hardie, in close alliance with Palmer's son, arranged a comprehensive exhibition of Palmer's work at the Victoria and Albert Museum in 1926, and had an enviable chance of seeing and selecting much material little known at the time. Of the Shoreham drawings he writes that "Palmer is telling you not what he has seen but of his thoughts—his thoughts of the glory of the sun, the magic of the moonlight, the mystery of the stars; thatched cottages, couched under immemorial trees; the enigmatic beauty of lanterns swinging in the night; lamplight giving gold to a window-blind; the goodness of harvest and ripe fruitage; men that drive the ground and scatter the grain; all the bounty and beauty that make the history and happiness of rural England."

Palmer made sketching tours to Devonshire and North Wales, then in 1838 he married Linnell's eldest daughter, Hannah, and departed to Italy for his honeymoon. He still had over forty years of life before him but the inspiration which had produced the Shoreham drawings was gone.

He was elected to membership of the Water-colour Society in 1843. During the later years of his life he successfully took up etching. In 1861 he moved from his Kensington home and in the following year settled at Redhill near his father-in-law. Palmer appears to have had a distressing relationship with Linnell. They differed over religious opinions and Linnell's Victorian "manliness" ill-matched Palmer's sensitive, slightly bohemian manner. Palmer became increasingly ill with asthma toward the end of his life and died on 24 May 1881, while his old friend George Richmond sat reading prayers beside his bed.

138 AT HAILSHAM, SUSSEX: A STORM APPROACHING, 1821

Watercolor. 8 5/16 x 12½ inches (21.2 x 31.8 cm.)

Inscribed: *At Hailsham / SP* lower left, and *1821 Sussex* upper right. Verso, inscribed by A. H. Palmer *Picture for the sketch exhibited at the British Institution 1822 'Storm Coming On.' Life and Letters Catalogue p. 407. This sketch was made before Samuel Palmer knew John Linnell.*

Provenance: A. H. Palmer; L. G. Duke (D.33), sold Sotheby's 29 April 1971, lot 115 (ill.); John Baskett 1971.

Literature: Martin Hardie, *Samuel Palmer*, Old Water-colour Society's Club, vol. IV, 1927, pl. x; Geoffrey Grigson, *Samuel Palmer, The Visionary Years*, 1947, no. 18, pl. 6; Adrian Bury, *Two Centuries of British Water-colour Painting*, 1950, pp. 21–22, p. 115; Martin Hardie, II, p. 161, pl. 144.

Exhibited: Victoria and Albert Museum, *Samuel Palmer*, 1926, no. 49, pl. xv; Royal Scottish Academy, Edinburgh, 1945; Southampton Art Gallery, *English Landscape*, 1951, no. 50; Arts Council, *Samuel Palmer and his Circle*, 1957, no. 1.

139 MOONLIT SCENE WITH A WINDING RIVER

Pen, ink, and brown wash heightened with white. 10½ x 7⅛ inches (26.5 x 18.2 cm.)

Provenance: A. H. Palmer; sold Christie's 4 March 1929; T. E. Lowinsky; Justin Lowinsky 1963.

Literature: Geoffrey Grigson, *Samuel Palmer, The Visionary Years*, 1947, p. 168, no. 55, pl. 22; Martin Hardie, ii, pl. 154.

Exhibited: Victoria and Albert Museum, *Samuel Palmer*, 1926, no. 60; Royal Academy, *British Art*, 1934, no. 893 (ill.); Colnaghi, 1964–65, and Yale University Art Gallery, 1965, no. 19, pl. ix.

Circa 1827.

140 A COW LODGE WITH A MOSSY ROOF

Pen, ink, watercolor, and gouache. 10½ x 14¾ inches (26.7 x 37.2 cm.)

Provenance: Howard Wright; Col. Bertram Buchanan; Mrs. Peter Pardoe, sold Sotheby's 20 November 1963, lot 60 (ill.); Colnaghi 1963.

Literature: Geoffrey Grigson, *Samuel Palmer, The Visionary Years*, 1947, p. 173, no. 72, frontispiece.

Exhibited: Arts Council, *Samuel Palmer and his Circle*, 1956, no. 25.

Circa 1828–29.

141 THE VALLEY OF VISION

Pen and brown ink with gray wash heightened with white. 11 x 17¼ inches (28 x 44 cm.)

Provenance: A. H. Palmer; L. G. Duke (D.663); Colnaghi 1961.

Literature: Geoffrey Grigson, *Samuel Palmer, The Visionary Years*, 1947, p. 175, no. 82.

Exhibited: Victoria and Albert Museum, *Samuel Palmer*, 1926, no. 59; Eton College, *Loan Exhibition of English Drawings from the Collection of L. G. Duke*, 1948, no. 35; South London Art Gallery, *English Landscapes*, 1951, no. 51; City Museum and Art Gallery, Birmingham, 1954; British Council, *British Water-colours for Switzerland*, 1955–56, no. 80; Arts Council, *Samuel Palmer and his Circle*, 1957, no. 20 (ill.); Arts Council, *The Romantic Movement*, 1959, no. 800; National Gallery, Washington, 1962, no. 48 (ill.); V.M.F.A., Richmond, 1963, no. 188; Colnaghi, 1964–65, and Yale University Art Gallery, 1965, no. 20; Victoria, 1971, no. 27.

Circa 1829–30. The old tithe barn features in several of Palmer's drawings made when he was staying at Shoreham.

142 UNDERRIVER HILLS, NEAR SEVENOAKS, KENT, FROM THE GROUNDS OF J. HERRIES ESQ.

Watercolor. 9½ x 14 inches (24 x 35.5 cm.)

Provenance: Fine Art Society 1967.

Circa 1833–35.

Pen and watercolor heightened with white, on brown paper. 14⅞ x 18¾ inches (37.9 x 47.5 cm.)

Inscribed: *Mount Siabod from Tyn-y-Coed near Capel Curig. on the road to Bettws-y-Coed* lower right.

Provenance: Mrs. Arthur Davey, granddaughter of Palmer's friend George Richmond, R.A.; Martin Hardie; Colnaghi 1961.

Literature: Geoffrey Grigson, *Samuel Palmer, The Visionary Years*, 1947, p. 132, pl. 67; Martin Hardie, II, p. 162.

Exhibited: British Council, Scandinavia, *British Painting, 1790–1850*, 1949–50, no. 71; British Council, *English Water-colours for Switzerland, 1955–56*, no. 87; Durlacher Galleries, New York, *Samuel Palmer*, 1949; Graves Art Gallery, Sheffield, *Samuel Palmer*, 1961, no. 40; National Gallery, Washington, 1962, no. 49; V.M.F.A., Richmond, 1963, no. 190; Colnaghi, 1964–65, and Yale University Art Gallery, 1965, no. 22.

Drawn on one of Palmer's tours of North Wales in 1835 or 1836. In a letter dated 19 August 1836, written from Tintern to George Richmond, Palmer mentions a visit to Snowdon and asks for a loan of three pounds to get him back to London, adding "If you've a mangy cat to drown, christen it Palmer." The drawing, one of a group which descended to George Richmond's granddaughter, may have been a thank-offering for the loan.

John Frederick Lewis, R.A. (1805–1876)

Lewis was born in London, the eldest son of Frederick Charles Lewis, painter and engraver, from whom he had early tuition in drawing. As a young man he had a talent for painting animals, and the family's friendship with the Landseers must have helped to develop this. He had early successes in exhibiting: one of his animal paintings was bought by George Garrard, R.A., among the best painters of animals at that time. When he was fifteen, Lewis worked as assistant to Sir Thomas Lawrence, sketching animals and backgrounds to portrait paintings. At nineteen he published *Studies of Wild Animals*, a set of etched and mezzotinted plates, done with great skill; and royal employment followed this, with George IV engaging him to paint deer and sporting subjects at Windsor. After a tour in North Italy he worked in England for some five years. The President of the Water-colour Society, George Robson, encouraged Lewis to change his medium from oil to watercolor. In 1827 he was elected Associate of the Society and became President twenty-eight years later.

Lewis lived in Spain from 1832 to 1834, and on his return to England published lithographs of his Spanish drawings. From 1837 onwards for thirteen years he traveled extensively with no interval in England. France, Italy, Malta, Corfu, Albania, Greece, Asia Minor were countries he toured first; but Egypt claimed him for almost the whole of ten years. He adopted the life, dress, and manners of that country "like a languid lotus-eater," to quote from a long and graphic account given by his friend Thackeray, who met Lewis in Cairo in 1844. But this

101

long absence came to an end seven years later when Lewis married an English girl in Cairo and, predictably, returned to England forthwith. When his work reappeared at exhibitions, his name was not generally known, and he was hailed by some as a new discovery. He himself told Holman Hunt that he found English art in the "woefullest condition" on his return and that he had decided to revert to oil-painting. Lewis was elected Associate of the Royal Academy in 1859 and Royal Academician in 1865. He died on 15 August 1876 at Walton-on-Thames.

144 STUDY OF A LIONESS

Watercolor. 14⅜ x 16⅝ inches (36.5 x 42.2 cm.)
Provenance: John, Lord Northwick; A. P. Oppé; T. Girtin; Tom Girtin; John Baskett 1970.
Literature: Martin Hardie, III, pl. 69.
Exhibited: Royal Academy, *The Girtin Collection*, 1962, no. 85.

A menagerie at Exeter Exchange in the Strand was a haunt of Lewis' as a young man. Among his early etchings were several versions of a lion's head, and this drawing was probably his working study for them.

145 BEDOUIN ARABS

Watercolor and body color on buff paper. 13¾ x 20⅜ inches (35 x 51.7 cm.)
Provenance: P. J. Henry; Colnaghi 1962.
Exhibited: V.M.F.A., Richmond, 1963, no. 443.

On his return to England from the Near East, Lewis made many compositions such as this. They were termed "Egyptian social scenes" by Holman Hunt. The "Arabs" look somewhat west of East and could probably be dubbed with identities from Lewis' circle of friends. The drawing is one of the best in examples showing exotic figures in exquisite surroundings drawn with superfine lines in rich coloring; such works have called for superlatives from all who have written about Lewis.

Edward Lear (1812–1888)

Lear was born in Holloway, London, on 12 May 1812, the youngest but one of the twenty-one children of Jeremiah Lear, a stockbroker who fell into debt in 1816. Lear was brought up and largely educated by his eldest sister, Anne. Having taught himself to draw by making minutely detailed studies of birds, flowers, insects, and seashells, he received his first regular employment making drawings for the Zoological Society. At twenty, he published his *Illustrations of the Family of Psittacidae, or Parrots*, and went on to make drawings for the zoologists Bell and Gray and the ornithologist John Gould. Gray recommended him to Lord Derby, a keen naturalist with a private menagerie at Knowsley Hall. There Lear worked from 1832 to 1836, making drawings to illustrate *Gleanings from the Menagerie and Aviary at Knowsley Hall* (privately printed, 1846), with notes "gleaned" by Gray from Lord Derby's records. In the benevolent atmosphere of Lord Derby's household another of Lear's talents flowered: while he meticulously painted the Whiskered Yarke, the Eyed Tyrse, and the Eyebrowed Rollulus he composed, for the entertainment of Lord Derby's grandchildren, grandnephews, and grandnieces, the limericks which were eventually published in his first *Book of Nonsense* (1846).

Landscape painting, which was to become the mainstay of Lear's career, appears first seriously to have engaged his attention during a tour of the Lake District in 1835. Ill-health (he suffered from bronchitis, asthma, and the epilepsy which, in the form of *le petit mal*, dogged him throughout his life) inclined him to residence abroad; and in the summer of 1837 he departed for Italy. An innate restlessness drew him henceforth ceaselessly to wander, back and forth from England to France, Switzerland, Germany, and the Low Countries; Italy, Sicily, Corsica, and the Balkans; Egypt and the Far East; India and Ceylon. Wherever he went, he drew. His output was prodigious (there are over 3,400 landscape drawings in the Harvard collection alone). His preferred subjects have been summarized by Brian Reade as "dramatic and associative . . . far horizons, sheer precipices, towering trees, lonely ruins"; his preferred atmosphere was a hot stillness. His invariable procedure was to make rapid, preliminary sketches on the spot, annotated with whimsically spelled notes of detail and color, later to be "penned out" to completion, often copied and recopied. His coloring at its best is, in Philip Hofer's words, "sparing, sober and subtle."

Lear wrote and illustrated seven books recording his travels. His *Illustrated Excursions in Italy* (1846) so impressed Queen Victoria that she summoned him to give her a course of twelve drawing lessons ("Mr. Lear . . . teaches remarkably well"). Lear himself in later life took lessons in oil-painting from Holman Hunt, but his work in this medium is comparatively heavy. He published three further books of nonsense, and was renowned for these long before he was seriously appreciated as a landscape painter.

Lear's life was a constant battle against financial difficulties and poor health. He overcame them by a sense of humor and an appetite for work. He described himself as "sociable but not gregarious." He made numerous friends, to whom he was a witty and prolific correspondent. It must indeed have been "pleasant to know Mr. Lear." He died unmarried, at San Remo, Italy, on 29 January 1888.

146 A WEASEL

Watercolor. 7⅜ x 11 inches (18.7 x 27.9 cm.)

Inscribed: E. Lear. del. / August. 29th. 1832 below branch, and on verso *Mustela Putorius female / August 29 1832.*

Provenance: Abbott and Holder 1971.

Dated 1832, this drawing was made at a time when the twenty-year-old Lear was chiefly working for Lord Derby on a series of drawings, some of which were used to illustrate *Gleanings from the Menagerie and Aviary at Knowsley Hall*, and is very similar in treatment to the *Lemur Rufus* or the *Quebec Marmot* in that work. In his Preface to it, J. E. Gray, then Assistant Keeper in the Zoological Department of the British Museum, wrote of Lear's drawings that "their chief value consists in their being accurate representations of living specimens." The artist's power of observation and the extremely fine brushwork with which he suggests sleek fur may, however, be equally relished by non-zoologists. *Mustela putorius* is the European polecat, sometimes called the fitchet weasel.

147 WIED ZURRIK

Watercolor. 10 x 13¾ inches (25.5 x 35 cm.)

Inscribed: *Wied Zurrik. / 11 March . 10 AM. (121)* lower right; *sea dark / purple gray* center.

Provenance: Mrs. Lloyd Browne; Agnew 1967.

The inscriptions on Lear's drawings are frequently phonetically spelled, but are usually precisely dated. "Zurrik" is Zurrieq in Malta (*wied* meaning ravine). It is unlike Lear not to have added the year to the hour, the day, and the month. He visited Malta many times; possibly this drawing was made during the winter of 1865–66 which Lear spent in the island, declaring by March that he had "drawn all Malta."

William Callow (1812–1908)

Callow was born on 28 July 1812. His long, successful, and serene life as an artist began when he was eleven, coloring prints for Theodore Fielding. At seventeen he was in Paris, employed by an engraver on Fielding's recommendation. In 1831 he became a friend of Thomas Shotter Boys, whose studio he shared two years afterwards. Callow recalls making some large sketches for Boys from the bridges in Paris, for which he was paid in books. Success mounted for Callow when he was chosen as drawing-master to the children of Louis Philippe, as the result of his exhibits at the Paris Salon. A gold medal was awarded him by the Salon in 1840, the year he started his extensive travels in Europe.

On his return to England he became a constant exhibitor at the Water-colour Society; his exhibits amounted to some 1500 drawings during the seventy years he was a member.

Callow's best work was done before 1850, especially drawings painted with the inspiration from Bonington that he absorbed through Boys. The *Pont Neuf* shows this clearly, and it may have been based on one of the drawings he made for Boys. Later watercolors, although skillful and well composed, have little of this former brilliance.

Callow died at Great Missenden, Buckinghamshire, on 20 February 1908.

148 LE PONT NEUF, PARIS

Watercolor. 13 x 19⅜ inches (33 x 49.2 cm.)

Inscribed: *W. Callow* lower right.

Provenance: Agnew 1971.

Exhibited: Victoria, 1971, no. 2, pl. i.

Richard Dadd (1817–1886)

Dadd was born on 1 August 1817 at Chatham, the son of Robert Dadd, a chemist and geologist. He received a conventional training as an artist at the Royal Academy schools. He first exhibited at the Royal Academy in 1839. Two years earlier he had gathered round him an informal group of young fellow-artists who called themselves "The Clique". The other members were Augustus Egg, O'Neil, "Spanish" Phillip, and Frith. At this time Dadd secured an important commission from Lord Foley for the decoration of his house: a series of over one hundred paintings to depict scenes to illustrate Tasso's *Jerusalem Delivered* and Byron's *Manfred*. He exhibited annually at the Academy until 1842, when he left for the Near East with Sir Thomas Phillips. The journey, which he hoped would provide him with material for the rest of his life, took him to Venice, Bologna, Corfu, Athens, Damascus, Baalbek, and Thebes, returning through Malta, Naples, Rome, and Paris. Afterwards, Dadd engaged himself on a design of St. George for the competition for the decoration of the Houses of Parliament.

In 1843, the illness which had been growing on him—a form of schizophrenia—brought him to total breakdown. His father took him on a visit to the country to obtain the quiet advised by Dr. Sutherland, chief physician at St. Luke's Asylum and an expert on mental disorders. On the evening of their arrival at Cobham, near Gravesend, Dadd murdered his father and fled to France, where he was apprehended near Fontainebleau trying to cut the throat of a fellow traveler. He was extradited from France after nearly a year and removed, without the unhappy experience of a trial, to Bethlem, the mental hospital in St. George's Fields, Lambeth, to be detained indefinitely.

After some twenty years, he was transferred in 1864 to the newly opened Broadmoor Criminal Lunatic Asylum. The illness, and his creative imagination, appear to have abated during the later years of his life. He contracted tuberculosis and died in one of the infirmaries at Broadmoor on 8 January 1886.

149 THE PASSION OF TREACHERY

Pen and watercolor, heightened with white. 14 x 9¾ inches (35.2 x 24.7 cm.)

Inscribed: *Sketch to illustrate the Passions / Treachery. by Richd Dadd— / Bethlem Hospital London. 1853*, lower left.

Provenance: Durlacher 1962.

Dadd made a series of drawings to illustrate the Passions. The earliest date from 1853, and they continue at regular intervals throughout 1854 and 1855, and thereafter less frequently. The subjects may have been suggested to him by William Hood, the Resident Physician appointed to Bethlem in 1852, who appears to have taken a particular interest in his unusual patient.

Eleven of the drawings from this series are still in the possession of the Bethlem Royal Hospital and vary a great deal in quality. Many, however, are yellowy brown in tone, and all the figures are characterized by blazing eyes.

John Ruskin (1819–1900)

Ruskin was born in London on 8 February 1819, the only child of a prosperous sherry merchant who continuously provided encouragement and financial independence for his talented son. Ruskin was a solitary and precocious child, showing early evidence of powerful intellect of a kind which, not itself imaginatively creative, takes pleasure in analyzing, describing, and teaching. Throughout his life he delighted in drawing; but he was only twenty-one when he saw clearly that he would never become a great artist, and that his vocation lay rather in interpretation: "The end of study in us who are not to be artists is . . . to receive what I am persuaded God means to be the *second* source of happiness to man—the impression of that mystery which . . . we call 'beauty'." Ruskin became the greatest English art critic of his age. He was a prolific writer, whose collected works number thirty-nine volumes; a stimulating lecturer, whether to workingmen's colleges or as Slade Professor of Fine Art at Oxford; a social reformer who championed, among other causes, a system of national education; and a generous donor, who dispersed the large fortune inherited from his father in charitable and philanthropic projects. His life, though full, was rarely happy, and from 1875 he became increasingly prey to mental derangement which finally incapacitated him in 1889. He died at Coniston in the Lake District on 20 January 1900.

The greatest single enthusiasm of Ruskin's life was his admiration of Turner. For his thirteenth birthday he was given a copy of Rogers' *Italy*, with engravings after Turner which he set himself to copy in minutest detail; as a young man he already owned several Turner watercolors, and with his father's help was to build up a large collection of them. Shortly after taking his degree at Oxford, he read a review ridiculing Turner's pictures, and at once set to work on *Modern Painters*, of which the first volume was published anonymously in 1843. The book set out to demonstrate that Turner was "the only great man whom the school [of modern landscape] has produced." About Constable's art he was dismissive; he had little or nothing to say about J. R. Cozens, Hearne, Dayes, Girtin, Bonington, or Cotman, though praising lesser men such as Copley Fielding, William Hunt, Harding, and Nesfield. The book became a classic, but Ruskin himself later deprecated its "nasty, snappish, impatient, half-familiar, half-claptrap web of young-mannishness." Ruskin's partisanship embarrassed Turner, who growled at his young admirer that he "didn't know how difficult it is."

Ruskin's drawings are the expression, in fine line, of what Sir Kenneth Clark calls his "steady penetrating gaze": he "stared fixedly at details all his life." He taught himself to draw by copying Samuel Prout's drawings, and engravings after Turner, and had some lessons from Copley Fielding and J. D. Harding; later, on yearly holidays on the Continent with his parents, he took the drawings of David Roberts as his model, realizing that attempts to paint in Turner's style would be presumptuous. He continued to draw almost daily throughout his life, lovingly recording trees, skies, grasses, or architectural details. "There is a strong instinct in me," he wrote to his father in 1852, "to draw and describe the things I love—not for reputation, nor for the good of others, nor for my own advantage, but a sort of instinct like that for eating and drinking."

150 A VIEW OF BADEN IN SWITZERLAND

Pen and pencil with gray wash on buff paper, heightened with white and yellow and touched with watercolor. 11 $\frac{7}{16}$ x 14$\frac{5}{8}$ inches (29.1 x 37.2 cm.)
Provenance: Richard S. Nickson; John Baskett 1968.

This drawing may have been made during a tour of Switzerland which Ruskin made with his parents in 1854; Ruskin had a vague plan of producing a history of Switzerland illustrated with engravings from his own drawings of Geneva, Fribourg, Basle, Thun, Baden, and Schaffhausen, but completed few of the drawings.

PLATES

1 Jacques Le Moyne de Morgues *A Young Daughter of the Picts*

2   Isaac Oliver   *Leda and the Swan*

3   Inigo Jones   *Head of a Boy*

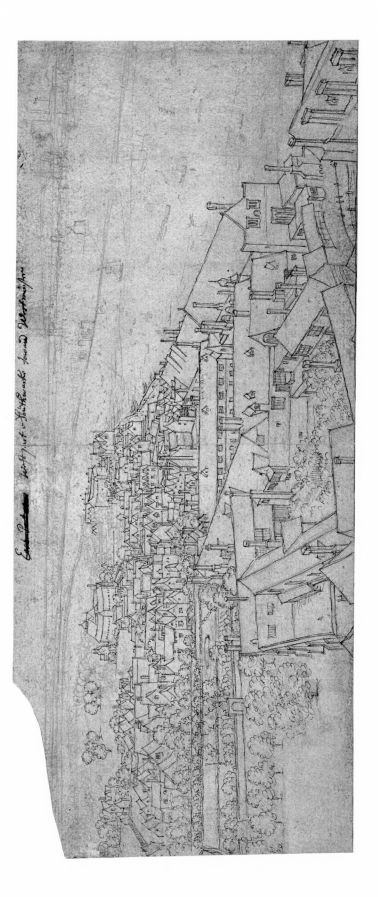

4   Wenceslaus Hollar   *London from Bankside*

5 Wenceslaus Hollar *Steiereck on the Danube*

6   William Faithorne   *Portrait of a Lady*

7   Thomas Wyck   *The Waterhouse and Old St. Paul's*

8 Francis Barlow *Hare Hunting*

9 Sir Godfrey Kneller *John Locke*

10　Jonathan Richardson I　*Young Man with Long Hair*

11   Sir James Thornhill   *Design for Ceiling, Walls, and Staircase*

12   John Wootton   *Hounds in a Landscape*

13   Marcellus Laroon II   *Lovers in a Glade*

14 Bernard Lens III *Long Water, Hampton Court Palace*

15 Antonio Canaletto *The Thames from York Stairs*

16 Antonio Canaletto *Old Walton Bridge, 1755*

17 William Hogarth *Subscription Roll for the Foundling Hospital, 1739*

18   William Hogarth   *The Industrious 'Prentice out of his Time*

19   William Hogarth   *The Industrious 'Prentice Married*

The best Manners is to give the least Trouble
& not to be too Ceremonious

20   James Seymour   *Sheet of Sketches*

21 Samuel Scott *A Ship's Boat*

22   William Taverner   *Landscape; possibly at Richmond, Surrey*

23   Francis Hayman, R.A.   *Figures Playing Shuttlecock*

24 Allan Ramsay *Head of a Girl*

25 Richard Wilson, R.A. *Temple of Minerva Medici, Rome, 1754*

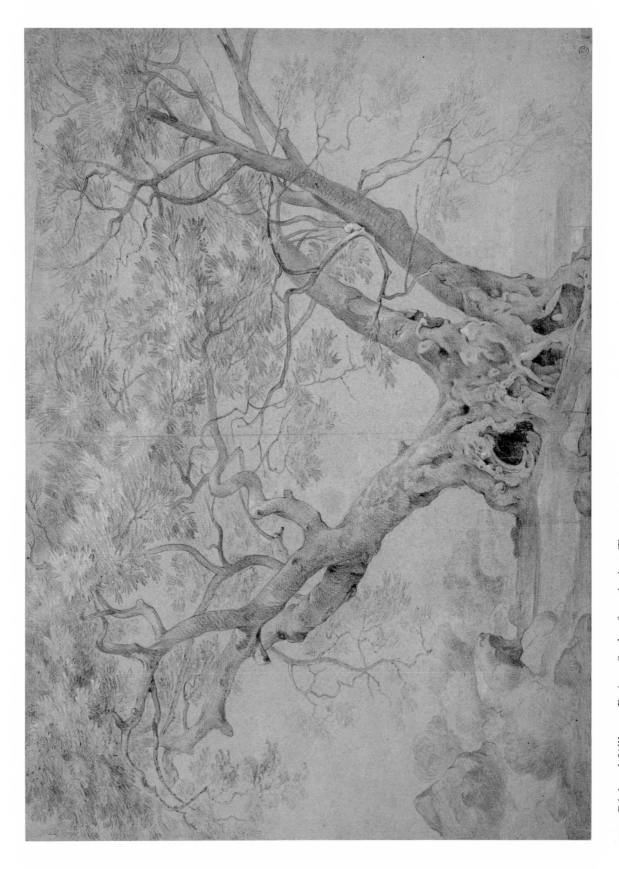

26 Richard Wilson, R.A. *Study of an Ancient Tree*

27 Alexander Cozens *Mountainous Landscape*

28   Thomas Sandby, R.A.   *Whitehall Showing Holbein's Gate*

29　Thomas Sandby, R.A.　*St. Paul's, Covent Garden*

30   Sir Joshua Reynolds, P.R.A.   *Study for a Self-Portrait*

31 George Stubbs, A.R.A. *Study for a Self-Portrait*

32 George Stubbs, A.R.A. *Horses Fighting*

33 George Stubbs, A.R.A. *A Prancing Horse*

34 Thomas Gainsborough, R.A. *Wooded Landscape with Gypsy Encampment*

35 Thomas Gainsborough, R.A. *Landscape with Horsemen and Covered Cart*

36   Thomas Gainsborough, R.A.   *Wooded Landscape with Figures*

37   Thomas Gainsborough, R.A.   *Study of Rocks and Plants*

38　Paul Sandby, R.A.　*The Norman Gate, Windsor Castle*

39 Paul Sandby, R.A. *Rosslyn Castle, North Berwick*

40   Paul Sandby, R.A.   *An Encampment in St. James's Park*

41 Paul Sandby, R.A. *Wakefield Lodge in Whittlebury Forest, 1767*

42 George Romney *Figures Fleeing from a City in Flames*

43 Jonathan Skelton *Harbledown, near Canterbury, 1757*

44　Francis Towne　*Grotto at Posilippo, Naples, 1781*

45   William Marlow   *The Amphitheatre at Nîmes*

46   John Hamilton Mortimer, A.R.A.   *Back View of the Artist*

Augt. 3. 1793

Geo Dance

47   George Dance II, R.A.   *Portrait of a Boy, 1793*

48   Henry Fuseli, R.A.   *Ariadne Watching Theseus with the Minotaur*

49   Henry Fuseli, R.A.   *Standing Woman*

50   William Pars, A.R.A.   *Rome from the Pincian, 1776*

51   Michael "Angelo" Rooker, A.R.A.   *Greyfriars Monastery, Winchester*

52 Thomas Hearne *View from Skiddaw*

53   Francis Wheatley, R.A.   *Donnybrook Fair, 1782*

54   Thomas Malton II   *The Royal Terrace, Adelphi*

55   Thomas Daniell, R.A.   *Some-Cheon on French Island*

56 John "Warwick" Smith *Villa Medici, Rome*

57 John Downman, A.R.A. *Mrs. Ives of Catton, 1780*

58 John Webber, R.A. *Landscape in Derbyshire*

59   John Brown   *The Geographers*

60   John Robert Cozens   *Lake of Albano and Castel Gandolfo*

61 John Robert Cozens *The Pays de Valais*

62   John Robert Cozens   *Near Chiavenna in the Grisons*

63   John Robert Cozens   *On the Lake of Nemi*

64 John Robert Cozens *Il Parco degli' Astroni*

65 John Raphael Smith *The Charmer*

66   Thomas Stothard, R.A.   *Design for a Silver Chalice*

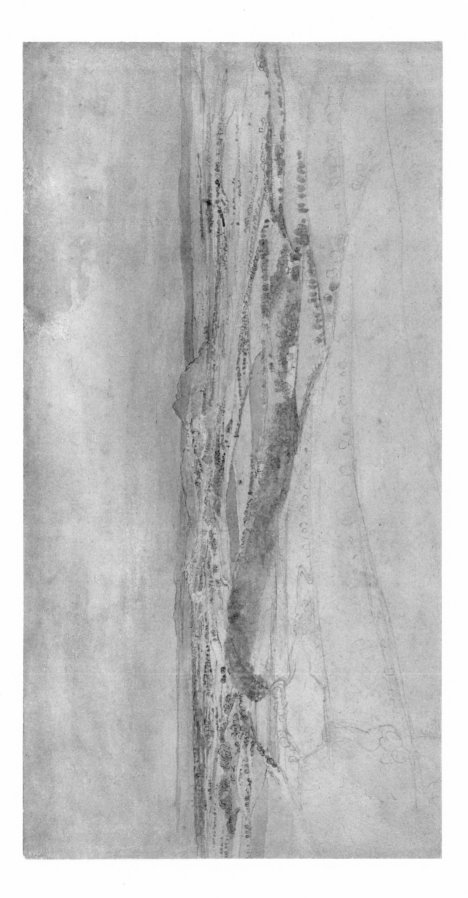

67   Thomas Stothard, R.A.   *A Distant View of Edinburgh, 1809*

68 Samuel Howitt *A Coach Passing through Chippenham*

69   Thomas Rowlandson   *A Review in the Market Place, Winchester*

70 Thomas Rowlandson *A Worn-out Debaucher*

71　Thomas Rowlandson　*Old Vauxhall Gardens*

72   Thomas Rowlandson   *A Horse Sale at Hopkins' Repository*

73 Thomas Rowlandson *The Picnic*

74   William Blake   *Tiriel Supporting Myratana*

ODE

ON THE DEATH OF A

FAVOURITE CAT.

Drowned in a Tub of Gold Fishes.

D 3

75 William Blake *Midst the Tide Two Angel Forms*

6
58 ODE ON A DISTANT PROSPECT
Theirs buxom Health, of rofy hue,
Wild wit, Invention ever-new,
And lively Cheer of Vigour born;
The thoughtlefs day, the eafy night,
The fpirits pure, the flumbers light,
That fly th' approach of morn.
Alas! regardlefs of their doom,
The little victims play!
No fenfe have they of ills to come,
Nor care beyond to-day:
Yet fee, how all around 'em wait
The minifters of human fate,
And black Misfortune's baleful train!
Ah, fhow them where in ambufh ftand,
To feize their prey, the murderous band!
Ah, tell them they are men!
Thefe fhall the fury paffions tear,
The vultures of the mind,
Difdainful

76 William Blake *The Vultures of the Mind*

85   THE PROGRESS OF POESY.

O'er her warm cheek, and rising bosom, move
The bloom of young desire, and purple light
       of Love.

II. 1.

Man's feeble race what ills await!
Labour, and Penury, the racks of Pain,
Disease, and Sorrow's weeping train,
And Death, sad refuge from the storms of Fate!
The fond complaint, my song, disprove,
And justify the laws of Jove.
Say, has he given in vain the heav'nly Muse?
Night, and all her sickly dews,
Her spectres wan, and birds of boding cry,
He gives to range the dreary sky:
Till down the eastern cliffs afar
Hyperion's march they spy, and glitt'ring
       shafts of war.

II. 2.

77   William Blake   *Hyperion's March*

78 William Blake *Prone on the Lowly Grave*

79   William Blake   *The Wise and Foolish Virgins*

80 Julius Caesar Ibbetson *The Sailor's Farewell, 1801*

81 Edward Francis Burney *The Triumph of Music*

82 Edward Dayes *Queen Square, London, 1786*

83　William Alexander　*City of Lin-Tsin, Shantung*

84   William Alexander   *The Dinner in Mote Park, Maidstone, 1799*

85   Joshua Cristall   *A Peasant Girl, 1812*

86 John Crome *A Boatload*

87 Robert Hills *A Village Snow Scene, 1819*

88   Henry Edridge, A.R.A.   *Stream with Trees and Cattle, 1807*

89 James Ward, R.A.   *Studies of Geese*

90   William Daniell, R.A.   *Windsor Castle, 1827*

91 Louis Francia *Mousehold Heath, Norwich, 1808*

92 George Chinnery, R.H.A. *Figure Seated by an Indian Temple*

93　Thomas Girtin　*The Ouse Bridge, York, 1800*

94 Thomas Girtin *The New Walk, York*

95   Thomas Girtin   *Lyme Regis*

96 Thomas Girtin *The Abbey Mill, Knaresborough*

97　Joseph Mallord William Turner, R.A.　*Newark-upon-Trent*

98 Joseph Mallord William Turner, R.A. *The Mer de Glace, Chamonix*

99   Joseph Mallord William Turner, R.A.   *Weymouth*

100   Joseph Mallord William Turner, R.A.   *Dartmoor: the Source of the Tamar and the Torridge*

101 Joseph Mallord William Turner, R.A.   *On the Washburn*

102 Joseph Mallord William Turner, R.A. *Leeds, 1816*

103 Joseph Mallord William Turner, R.A. *Vesuvius in Eruption, 1817*

104 Joseph Mallord William Turner, R.A. *Falls of the Reichenbach*

105 Joseph Mallord William Turner, R.A. *Patterdale*

106 Joseph Mallord William Turner, R.A. *Folkestone*

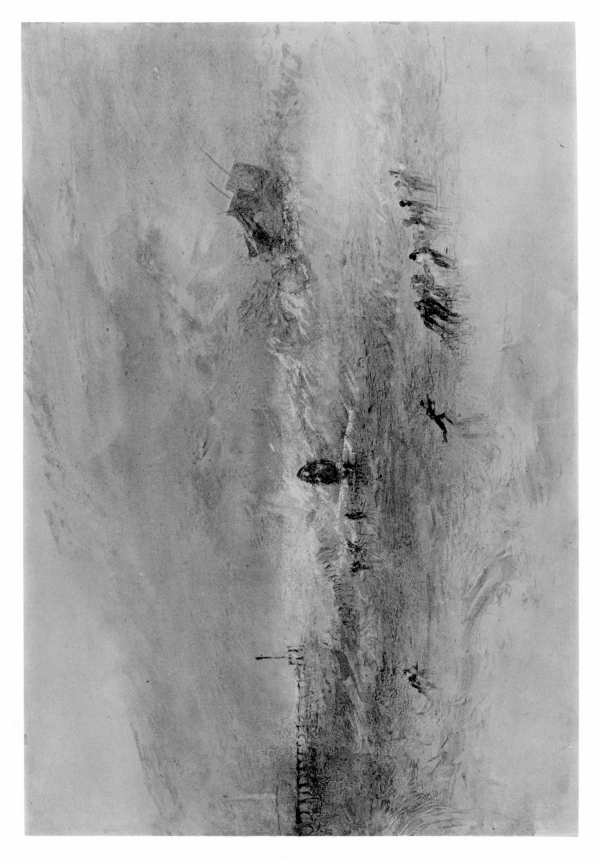

107   Joseph Mallord William Turner, R.A.   *Yarmouth Sands*

108 Joseph Mallord William Turner, R.A. *Venice*

109 Samuel Daniell *A Landscape in Ceylon*

110   John Constable, R.A.   *Landscape at East Bergholt*

111 John Constable, R.A. *Sky Study with Rainbow*

112 John Constable, **R.A.** *Fulham Church, 1818*

113   John Constable, R.A.   *Summer Landscape*

114　John Constable, R.A.　*Maria Constable* (?)

115   John Constable, R.A.   *Old Sarum in a Storm, 1828*

116　John Constable, R.A.　*Trees in a Meadow*

117   John Thirtle   *Landscape, possibly near Guildford*

118 John Varley *Conway, 1803*

119   John Varley   *Harlech Castle and Twgwyn Ferry, 1804*

120 Cornelius Varley "*Llyn Tally Llin at my Back*"

121 John Sell Cotman *Aberystwyth Castle*

122 John Sell Cotman *In Rokeby Park*

123   John Sell Cotman   *Domfront*

124 John Sell Cotman *Doorway and Window of a Church*

125 David Cox *Lancaster Sands*

126 Peter De Wint *The Old Bridge*

127 Peter De Wint *The Foss Dyke near Lincoln*

128   Sir David Wilkie, R.A.   *A Girl Wearing a Large Hat*

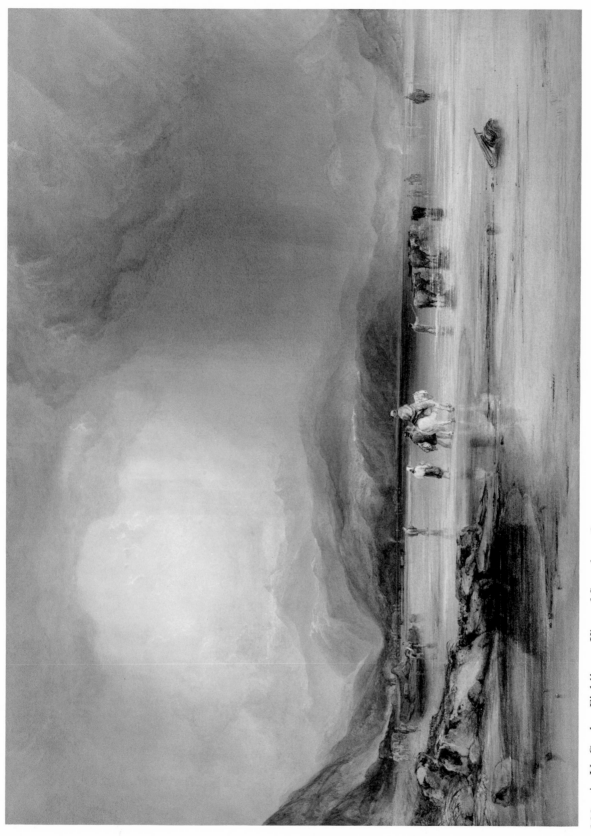

129 A. V. Copley Fielding *View of Snowdon, 1834*

130   William Turner of Oxford   *Donati's Comet, Oxford, 1858*

131 John Martin *The Thames, opposite Pope's Villa, 1850*

132   William Henry Hunt   *St. Martin-in-the-Fields*

133 John Linnell *Landscape in North Wales, 1813*

134   David Roberts, R.A.   *Karnac, 1838*

135   James Holland   *Coast Scene with Sailing Boats*

136   Richard Parkes Bonington   *Landscape with Windmills*

137　Thomas Shotter Boys　*L'Institut de France, Paris, 1830*

138   Samuel Palmer   *At Hailsham, Sussex, 1821*

139   Samuel Palmer   *Moonlit Scene with a Winding River*

140 Samuel Palmer *A Cow Lodge with a Mossy Roof*

141   Samuel Palmer   *The Valley of Vision*

142 Samuel Palmer *Underriver Hills, near Sevenoaks, Kent*

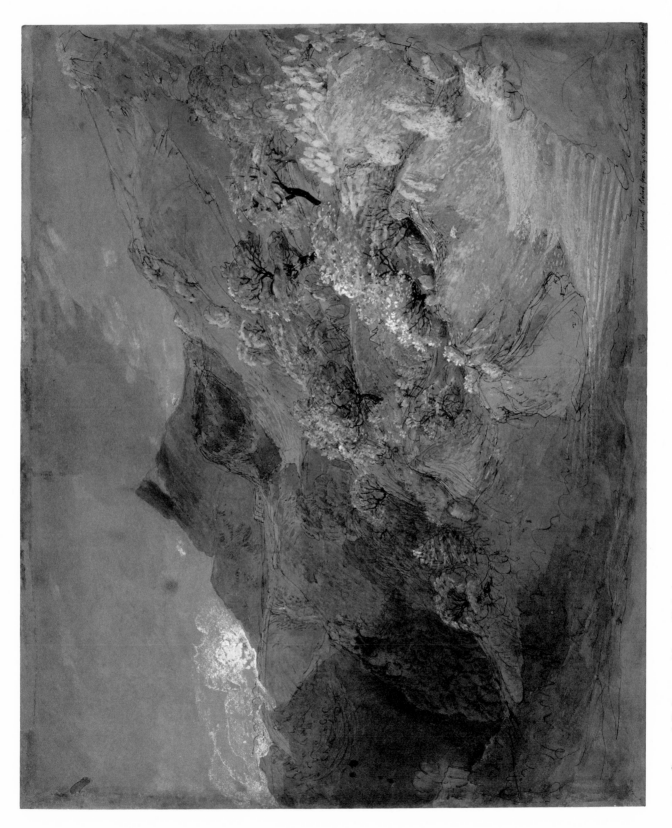

143 Samuel Palmer *Mount Siabod*

144   John Frederick Lewis, R.A.   *A Lioness*

145   John Frederick Lewis, R.A.   *Bedouin Arabs*

146 Edward Lear *A Weasel, 1832*

Wied Zurrik. 11 March. 10 A.M.

(121)

sea dark purple gray

147   Edward Lear   "*Wied Zurrik*"

148   William Callow   *Le Pont Neuf, Paris*

149 Richard Dadd *The Passion of Treachery, 1853*

150 John Ruskin *Baden, Switzerland*

Letterpress composition and printing by
THE STINEHOUR PRESS · LUNENBURG · VERMONT

Plates made and printed by
THE MERIDEN GRAVURE COMPANY · MERIDEN · CONNECTICUT

Binding by
NEW HAMPSHIRE BINDERY · CONCORD · NEW HAMPSHIRE

*

TYPOGRAPHY BY JOSEPH BLUMENTHAL

WITHDRAWN